North Korean Paradoxes

Circumstances, Costs,
and Consequences of
Korean Unification

Charles Wolf, Jr., Kamil Akramov

Prepared for the Office of the Secretary of Defense

 NATIONAL DEFENSE RESEARCH INSTITUTE

The research described in this report was prepared for the Office of the Secretary of Defense (OSD). The research was conducted in the RAND National Defense Research Institute, a federally funded research and development center supported by the OSD, the Joint Staff, the unified commands, and the defense agencies under Contract DASW01-01-C-0004.

Library of Congress Cataloging-in-Publication Data

Wolf, Charles, Jr.
    North Korean paradoxes : circumstances, costs and consequences of Korean
  unification / Charles Wolf, Jr., Kamil Akramov.
      p. cm.
    "MG-333."
    Includes bibliographical references.
    ISBN 0-8330-3762-5 (pbk. : alk. paper)
      1. Korean reunification question (1945–) 2. Korea (North)—Economic
  policy. 3. Korea (North)—Politics and government. 4. Security, International.
  I. Akramov, Kamil. II. Title.

DS917.444.W65 2005
951.9304'3—dc22

                                                              2005002942

The RAND Corporation is a nonprofit research organization providing objective analysis and effective solutions that address the challenges facing the public and private sectors around the world. RAND's publications do not necessarily reflect the opinions of its research clients and sponsors.

RAND® is a registered trademark.

Published 2005 by the RAND Corporation
1776 Main Street, P.O. Box 2138, Santa Monica, CA 90407-2138
1200 South Hayes Street, Arlington, VA 22202-5050
201 North Craig Street, Suite 202, Pittsburgh, PA 15213-1516
RAND URL: http://www.rand.org/
To order RAND documents or to obtain additional information, contact
Distribution Services: Telephone: (310) 451-7002;
Fax: (310) 451-6915; Email: order@rand.org

Preface

This monograph, focusing on North Korea, analyzes some of the economic, political, and security issues associated with Korean unification. The analysis considers the numerous puzzles and paradoxes that obscure the North Korean system, especially that system's structure and functioning as a "rent-seeking" economy. We also consider how the system might unravel, leading to the possibility of reunification, and what the attendant capital costs of reunification would be under differing circumstances and assumptions. Our estimates of these costs are then compared with those by other institutions and analysts.

Consideration is given to points of relevance and nonrelevance between the German experience with unification in the 1990s and that which might impend in Korea.

Finally, the monograph concludes by briefly assessing the problems that a reunified Korea would confront relating to possession of weapons of mass destruction, its relations with neighboring countries, especially China, and its alliance with the United States.

The monograph should be of interest and use to those in both the policy and scholarly communities concerned with Korea, and especially those concerned with the six-country talks in which the United States is periodically engaged with North Korea, South Korea, China, Japan, and Russia. The monograph should also be of interest to the business community, the media, and members of the larger public who follow developments in Northeast Asia.

This research was performed within the International Security and Defense Policy Center of the RAND National Research Defense Institute (NDRI), a federally funded research and development center sponsored by the Office of the Secretary of Defense, the Joint Staff, the unified commands, and the defense agencies.

Contents

Preface. iii
Figures vii
Tables ix
Summary. xi
Acknowledgments. xix
Acronyms xxi

CHAPTER ONE
Preamble: Purpose and Roadmap 1

CHAPTER TWO
North Korea: Obscurities and Paradoxes .3
Obscurities. 3
Paradoxes. 6

CHAPTER THREE
Size, Growth, and Structure of the North Korean Economy 9
Data Problems 9
The North Korean GDP 10
Structural Characteristics of North Korea's Economy 12

CHAPTER FOUR
How the System Might Unravel: Scenarios for Reunification. 21
Diminished Attention to Reunification 21
Three Reunification Scenarios 22

Scenario A: Unification Through System Evolution and
  Integration 22
Scenario B: Unification Through Collapse and Absorption 23
Scenario C: Unification Through Conflict 24

CHAPTER FIVE
**The Capital Costs of Korean Reunification: Estimation and
  Management** 27
Fluctuating Interest in Reunification 27
Simulation and Uncertainties 29
  The Model 30
  Simulation Results 37
  Distributing the Costs of Korean Reunification 42

CHAPTER SIX
Other Estimates of Reunification Costs 45
Differing Sources and Types of Cost Estimates 45
The Wide Range of Reunification Costs 46

CHAPTER SEVEN
Is Germany's Reunification Experience Relevant? 51
Germany's Reunification Costs 52
Germany's Military Unification Experience 54

CHAPTER EIGHT
Conclusions: Effects on Korean Security Policies and Programs 59
WMD Capabilities and Programs 60
Korea's Alliance with the United States 61

APPENDIX
A Simple Simulation Model for Sizing Korean Reunification Costs . . . 63

Bibliography 65

Figures

3.1. North Korea's Imports, Exports, and Trade Deficits,
1960–2001 16
5.1. Sensitivity of Cost Estimates to North Korea's
Preunification GDP 40
5.2. Sensitivity of Cost Estimates to Varying Incremental Capital
Coefficients 40
5.3. Sensitivity of Cost Estimates to Pace of Institutional
Reform 41
5.4. Sensitivity of Cost Estimates to Speed of Doubling North
Korea's GDP 41

Tables

3.1. North Korean and South Korean Gross Domestic Products, | 2002 11

3.2. North and South Korean GDP Growth Rates, 1990–2002 12

5.1. Incremental Capital-Output Ratios (ICOR) and GDP Growth in East Asian Countries 33

5.2. Estimates of Reunification Costs: Selected Simulation Results 39

6.1. Other Estimates of Reunification Costs 49

7.1. Military Forces and Military Burden in South and North Korea 57

Summary

The research on which this monograph is based addresses the circumstances, costs, and consequences of Korean reunification. All three of these issues involve large conceptual as well as empirical problems. The total costs of reunification would be dependent on how unification would occur, including, for example, the costs of meeting humanitarian demands, stabilization requirements, the needs of human capital reeducation training and replacement, and the demands of social integration.

Our focus here is on the capital costs of doubling the North Korean GDP in a short period of time (four to five years). This target is based on the arguable premise that such a rapid improvement would provide sufficient hope among the populace and stability in the polity to allow the embryonic unified regime to endure despite the persistence of substantial income and other disparities between North and South.

This premise does not deny that the regime would confront a wide range of other formidable challenges, burdens, and costs. A new government of a unified Korea would have to carefully manage these challenges and the continued existence of disparities to avoid excessive instability. We cite numerous examples and precedents in which unified, sovereign countries have managed to function and endure, notwithstanding the presence of enormous economic, social, and ethnic disparities and disharmonies.

Employing an aggregate, economy-wide simulation model, we find that the capital costs could vary widely from about $50 billion to

$670 billion (in 2003 dollars). Other costs mentioned above could vary even more widely, leading to large additional costs.

The report begins by examining the puzzles and paradoxes that obscure the North Korean system, how it functions, and how it manages to survive. Although it is one of 191 members of the United Nations, the lack of reliable information about it is unique among that group, not incidentally because the North Korean government ceased publishing information and data in the mid-1960s.

While the preeminent position of Kim Jong Il is apparently unchallenged, other aspects of North Korean politics remain obscure, including the relationship and interaction between Kim at the pyramid's top and the next levels in the military, technical, and managerial elites, and the respective roles and relative influence of these elites and of those of the North Korean People's Workers Party.

The North Korean economy is no less shrouded in obscurity than is the North Korean polity. The obscurities include whether the size of the North Korean economy is 1/50 or 1/25 the size of South Korea's economy or something in between, and whether annual GDP growth in the North has ranged between −6 and +6 percent, possibly averaging about −2 percent over the past dozen years, or instead has stagnated for most of this period.

Perhaps less obscure but still puzzling is North Korea's ability to maintain a huge military establishment including a consequential weapons development program and an overdeveloped defense industrial base, in the midst of the pervasive poverty and weak performance of the North Korean economy.

The monograph begins with an analysis of the North Korean economy based largely on data provided by South Korean sources. We estimate the size of the North Korean economy in 2002 at about US $17 billion at nominal foreign exchange rates or about $23 billion at purchasing power parity rates, compared with corresponding figures of $477 billion and $818 billion, respectively, for South Korea. Per capita income in North Korea in 2002 is estimated at $762 in nominal exchange rates and $1,021 at purchasing power parity rates, compared with figures of $10,000 and $15,500 per capita, respectively, in South Korea.

A central part of the North Korean economy's structure is the overdeveloped military sector, which includes the million-plus armed forces, defense research and development of nuclear and other weapons of mass destruction, and industrial production of conventional and unconventional weapons. In relation to the size of its population, North Korea's armed forces are the largest in Asia. In absolute terms, its armed forces are exceeded only by those of China, approximately matching those of India. Military spending and production by military industry represent between 15 percent and more than 30 percent of North Korea's GDP.[1]

Reflecting North Korea's priorities, military spending per active North Korean military personnel is between $3,900 and $5,500 depending on whether conversions are made at nominal exchange rates or purchasing power parity rates, respectively. The corresponding range for nonmilitary product per nonmilitary personnel is between $500 and $700. While military outlays are generally capital-intensive, the 8:1 ratio between per capita outlays for the military and non-military population in North Korea is extraordinarily high—about 50 percent higher than the roughly comparable figure in the United States.

One characteristic that is unique is what we have labeled North Korea's "rent-seeking" economic system. As a rent-seeking economy, the system relies on extracting some form of quasi-monopoly profits (or "rents") from its dealings with the rest of the world. While rent-seeking behavior is not unprecedented by other countries and business organizations, what is unique about North Korea's rent-seeking is that it focuses on specific activities insulated from normal market competition because the activities themselves are formally illegal, although enforcement of the laws is lax. Such are the circumstances surrounding North Korea's exports of drugs, counterfeit currencies, and various categories of weapons including missiles and nuclear weapons-related technology. North Korea's rent-seeking has perenni-

---

[1] The range reflects North Korean and foreign sources, respectively, with the upper end of the range from foreign sources, inclusive of some transfers to the military of fungible resources acquired from abroad.

ally followed a pattern of finding and exploiting these off-limits, extra-market niches. Data presented in this monograph suggest that North Korea's hard-currency rents from these various sources are relatively large. These rents provide centrally controlled resources whose disposition by Kim Jong Il ensures the fealty and support of the military, bureaucracy, and technocracy elites at the top of the system's pyramid. In turn, these elites exercise pervasive control over the masses of North Korea's population of approximately 22 million through a combination of repression, fear, and occasional benefactions.

Our summary of the North Korean system and how it operates serves as background for consideration of how the system might unravel. Especially since the demise of Kim Il Sung in 1994, observers have periodically conjectured that the North Korean regime's survival might be imperiled. However, in recent years these conjectures have receded for two reasons: First, North Korea's durability throughout this period seems to belie the credibility of scenarios envisaging the system's unraveling; second, the focus of external attention has drastically shifted away from conjectures about unraveling, concentrating instead on such immediate concerns as North Korea's repeated announcements and threats that it would reprocess spent nuclear fuel and/or enrich natural uranium to produce nuclear weapons.

In prior years, serious consideration was given to the possibility that the North Korean regime might collapse and reunification might impend. Observers were regularly surprised that this did not occur. Now, when relatively little attention is focused on possible unraveling and unification, surprise might be experienced in the reverse direction.

With this possibility in mind, we briefly consider three scenarios through which unification might occur:

- unification through system evolution and integration
- unification through collapse and absorption
- unification through conflict.

The monograph next turns to estimating the costs of possible Korean reunification, using for this purpose a simple simulation model with eight key parameters. The costs of reunification as estimated in this study are narrowly defined, focusing on the *incremental capital requirements* for doubling North Korea's GDP in a four- or five-year period. While this would be an ambitious and dramatic target, it cannot be construed as a proxy for all the challenges and problems that the newly configured government of a unified Korea would face. Nor would the capital costs of reaching this target suffice as an estimate of the total cost burden that a unified Korean government would face. As noted above, the noncapital costs would include the demands of humanitarian relief, political and job reeducation, administration replacement, and political and social integration. Moreover, these other costs could vary even more widely and lead to a larger burden than that imposed by capital costs alone. At the same time, as previously mentioned, it should be noted that many countries and governments have functioned and endured as unified entities with tolerable levels of stability while at the same time confronting deep political, cultural, religious, and economic burdens and disparities. Resolving these problems should not therefore be considered a precondition for unification.

It has been generally and not implausibly presumed that Korean reunification would impose larger relative cost burdens than have materialized in the case of German reunification. Reasons for this presumption are that relative income levels are much lower and the relative populations are much larger in the North Korean-South Korean comparison than in the East German-West German instance. Per capita GDP in North Korea is probably between 6 and 12 percent of that of South Korea, compared to 25–33 percent of East Germany's per capita GDP relative to that of West Germany in 1990.

However, several countervailing considerations may reduce the relative costs of Korean reunification and make them less forbiddingly high and gloomy than the foregoing story might imply. For example, the economic burden on North Korea from its huge military establishment has been vastly greater in relative terms than were the costs of East Germany's military establishment preceding German reunification. Thus, reunification in Korea might provide an opportunity for realizing resource savings by linking the *building-down* of the North Korean military to *building-up* the relatively small and deprived civilian capital base in North Korea. Moreover, it is probably true that prevailing attitudes and low labor productivity among the North Korean population as well as impediments imposed by Korea's physical geography would conduce to more limited population movement from North to South than that which preceded and accompanied German unification after the wall between East and West Germany came down. Hence, the anticipated surge of East Germans toward the West imposed a greater urgency on relieving the disparities between West and East German per capita income than might be necessary in the corresponding circumstances accompanying Korean reunification.

The simulation model used in this study to estimate the capital costs of rapidly doubling North Korea's GDP has been run several hundred times with varying combinations of the parameters reflecting differing aspects of the reunification scenarios referred to above. To reflect the huge uncertainties involved in estimating reunification costs, we allow for a range of different values for the key parameters: the pre- and postunification levels of GDP and military spending in the North and the South; the incremental capital-output ratio (ICOR) relating the investment requirements for raising output and income; the effectiveness of institutional reform encompassing marketization, property rights, and the rule of law; and whether the stipulated target for doubling GDP in the North is set at four or five years.

The capital costs of Korean unification as derived from the simulations and based on the stipulated economic growth target cover a range between $50 billion to nearly $670 billion in 2003 U.S. prices. If North Korea's initial GDP is as large as 8 percent of that of the South, then the capital costs of unification will tend toward the higher end of this range because the capital requirements for doubling output will be higher. If the initial North Korean GDP is lower relative to that of South Korea, the corresponding capital requirements for doubling output in the postunification North will be reduced. If the ICOR is as high as 5, the corresponding costs will be raised toward the higher end of the range. If the preunification military spending share of North Korea's GDP is relatively higher but is substantially reduced after reunification, then the savings from military build-down will be somewhat larger, and the residual capital costs of reunification will be lowered. Furthermore, these costs will vary inversely with whether the institutional reform strategy accompanying reunification is assumed to be effective, moderately effective, or relatively ineffective. If median values are posited for the various parameters, the estimated capital costs would be approximately $350 billion.

The monograph next considers various possibilities for distributing the resulting capital costs, dividing them among four components: private capital flows from South to North Korea; private capital flows from the rest of the world; public transfers from South Korea; and public transfers from the rest of the world. If, for example, private and public capital transfers from South Korea made up, say, one-third of the capital cost burden, the burden on the South's economy would span a range between $17 billion and $223 billion, representing between 0.9 percent and 11 percent, of South Korea's cumulative GDP over a four- or five-year period. The remaining capital costs could plausibly be shared among private and public sources in the United States, Japan, China, the European Union, and the international financial institutions. To further limit the cost burden, we briefly discuss an idea for demobilizing large elements of the North Korean military into a "civil construction corps" to provide a contract labor pool available for commercial and public employment by both private direct investors in North Korea and by the reunified Korean government.

While our estimates of the capital costs of reunification span a wide range, this range is narrower in dollars, and its absolute dollar magnitudes are substantially smaller than estimates made by other institutions and analysts. Those other estimates—no less fallible than our own—vary widely in the economic targets they adopt, the time horizons they cover, their baseline data assumptions, and the methodologies they employ. Consequently, they are not strictly comparable to our own or to one another, although each purports to measure something broadly construed as "the cost of Korean reunification." Their variation extends from $290 billion (an estimate made in 1994 and posited over a 32-year period) to $3.2 trillion (estimated in 1997 and extending over a 10-year period).

The monograph also assesses the relevance and nonrelevance of Germany's unification in the 1990s and that which might impend in Korea. This assessment suggests that the dissimilarities between the two cases are profound and pervasive, especially as concerns their economic and cost dimensions; some aspects of Germany's experience with military unification may have more relevance for the Korean case.

Finally, the monograph concludes with a brief consideration of some problems that a unified Korea would confront relating to possession of weapons of mass destruction, its relations with neighboring countries, especially China, and its alliance with the United States.

Acknowledgments

The authors appreciate the constructive comments on an earlier draft provided by reviewers Bruce Bennett at RAND, Nicholas Eberstadt at the American Enterprise Institute, and by Michael Walsh and Michael Finnegan in the Department of Defense. It goes without saying that none of them bears any responsibility for the analysis, judgments, or estimates we have made.

We are also pleased to acknowledge the efficient editorial assistance received from Miriam Polon, and the diligent logistic and computer assistance provided by Leah Gangelhoff in assembling and navigating through several earlier drafts.

Acronyms

ACDA	Arms Control and Disarmament Agency
CCC	civil construction corps
CLSA	Credit Lyonnais Societé Anonyme
CSIS	Center for Strategic and International Studies
FRG	Federal Republic of Germany
GDP	gross domestic product
GDR	German Democratic Republic
GNI	gross national income
GNP	Gross national product
ICOR	incremental capital-output ratio
IIE	Institute for International Economics
IISS	International Institute of Strategic Studies
IRS	institutional reform strategy
KDI	Korean Development Institute
KIEP	Korean Institute for Economic Policy
KNSO	(South) Korean National Statistical Office
LMS	Lund Macroeconomic Studies
MIT	Massachusetts Institute of Technology
NBER	National Bureau for Economic Research
OECD	Organization for Economic Cooperation and Develoment
OSD	Office of the Secretary of Defense
PSI	Proliferation Security Initiative
ROK	Republic of Korea
SIPRI	Stockholm International Peace Research Institute
WMD	weapons of mass destruction

CHAPTER ONE

Preamble: Purpose and Roadmap

The principal aim of this research is to analyze some of the central issues associated with Korean reunification—and especially its attendant costs. As essential background for the analysis, we begin in Chapters Two and Three with a brief examination of the structure and functioning of the North Korean system—what is known and not known about its various dimensions and particularly about its economy.

Chapter Four briefly summarizes how the system might unravel.

Chapter Five describes the simulations we have done to estimate the capital costs of reunification. The costs of reunification as estimated in this analysis are narrowly defined, focusing on the incremental capital requirements to double North Korea's GDP in a four- or five-year period. Our estimates include the costs of new plant and equipment, replacing existing but unproductive capital, and building infrastructure necessary to reach the specified macroeconomic growth targets. The estimates do *not* cover humanitarian, cultural, reeducational, and other social costs that would accompany reunification. Attempting to estimate these costs would be both difficult and elusive. Moreover, it can be argued that many and perhaps most of these burdens can be construed as appropriate priority tasks for a unified Korean government to discharge, rather than tasks to be accomplished before unification.

Notwithstanding the narrow definition of the covered costs, our estimates span a wide range reflecting the major uncertainties attached to the estimates. The simulation methodology is explained in Chapter Five and in the appendix.

Chapter Six summarizes estimates of unification costs that have been made in other studies, some of which employ differing definitions of costs as well as different methodologies from those described in Chapter Five.

Chapter Seven considers the relevance and nonrelevance of Germany's unification experience to possible Korean unification.

Finally, Chapter Eight concludes with brief observations about the effects of unification on some of the security policies and problems that would confront a postunification Korea.

CHAPTER TWO

North Korea: Obscurities and Paradoxes

Obscurities

North Korea is conspicuous if not unique among the 190 other members of the United Nations in the paucity of reliable information about it. The North Korean government has never published a statistical yearbook, and it essentially ceased publishing even fragmentary economic statistics in the early 1960s. Limited information and data and the unreliability of what is available result in obscurity and conjecture rather than knowledge about the political, economic, and military circumstances actually prevailing in North Korea.

Its *political obscurities* are pervasive. They include the bizarre, volatile, and perhaps calculating character and behavior of its leadership; the content and meaning of its *juche* (self-reliance) ideology; the mind-shaping role of the "Great Leader" legacy of Kim Il Sung and its interpretation and application by the "Dear Leader" incumbency of Kim Jong Il; the relationship and interaction between the Kim dynastic leadership and the next levels in the North Korean hierarchy—namely, the military, technical, and managerial elites; and the respective roles and relative influence of these elites as well as those of the North Korean People's Workers' Party in the country's decision-making.

To be sure, some of these obscurities can be explained and rationalized within the North Korean context. For example, the *juche* ideology and apotheosizing of the dynastic leadership can perhaps be understood and explained as abetting North Korea's internal control mechanisms and as manifestations of Korean nationalism. Whether such explanations attenuate or accentuate the obscure and bizarre character of North Korea's polity is debatable.

In sum, what we know about the polity and politics of North Korea is exceeded by what we do not know. When the North Korean regime first denied, then subsequently admitted, and then still later denied existence of its uranium enrichment program; and when it halted, and then (perhaps) resumed its nuclear weapons program by extracting plutonium from spent nuclear fuel as well as by enriching uranium, this shifting behavior as well as the truth content associated with it remained obscure. It is not surprising that multiple and uncorroborated conjectures have been advanced by putative experts to account for this behavior.

When the "Dear Leader" first welcomed Kim Dae Jung's "Sunshine Policy" in the Pyongyang summit meeting of 2000 and then subsequently repudiated it, another enigma emerged. Perhaps a plausible explanation was North Korea's initial acceptance of a $100,000,000 compliance fee from the South, which the North may have presumed would be a recurring subvention, although the South did not so intend it and did not renew it.

When North Korea asserted that any attempt by the United States and collaborating nations in the Proliferation Security Initiative (PSI) to enforce sanctions against North Korea's current or prospective weapons exports would constitute an "act of war" to which the North would respond aggressively, the precise meaning of the threat itself was obscure and the question of how best to respond to it baffling. The puzzle was not diminished by the fact that North Korea had made similar threats in the past.

The North Korean *economy,* with which this report is more directly concerned than with its politics, is no less shrouded in obscurity. Among the economic obscurities, for example, are such questions as whether the size of the North Korean economy is 3 percent or 6 percent that of South Korea, and whether the North's gross domestic product (GDP) per capita is 6 percent or 12 percent of South

Korea's—or instead is outside these limits entirely.[1] No less obscure and equally puzzling are conflicting data suggesting that over the past six or seven years annual GDP growth in the North has ranged between –6 and +6 percent—averaging over the past dozen years about –2 percent—or, instead, has stagnated for most of this period.[2]

Less obscure but still puzzling is North Korea's ability to maintain a huge *military* establishment—which includes a consequential weapons development program and a relatively overdeveloped defense industrial base in the midst of the pervasive poverty and weak performance of its economy. The North Korean military establishment absorbs between 20 percent and over 30 percent of the economy's Gross National Income (GNI), and its ability to sustain such a large military effort recalls the plight of and constraints on the Soviet Union's economy in sustaining the Soviet military establishment in the 1970s and 1980s.[3] Indeed, the North Korean economy displays many structural characteristics associated with those of its Soviet antecedent, with one major exception. North Korea has placed heavy reliance upon acquiring large unrequited subventions and rents from abroad.[4] In contrast, the Soviet economy was remarkably and self-destructively autarchic, while it transmitted large resource transfers abroad. Subventions were not provided *to* the Soviet Union, but *by* the Soviet Union to Eastern Europe, North Korea, Cuba, and other extensions of the then-Soviet empire.[5]

---

[1] See below, Chapter Three, pp. 9–11. South Korea's population is 47.1 million, that of North Korea approximately 22.4 million. Economist (2004).

[2] See below, Table 3.2, p. 12.

[3] Data on North Korea's military expenditures are derived from various sources including *SIPRI Yearbook*; IISS, the *Military Balance;* the U.S. Arms Control and Disarmament Agency's *World Military Expenditures and Arms Transfers Reports* until 1997 and the State Department thereafter; and South Korean government agencies and research institutes. However, these data vary because of differences in exchange rates, methods of statistical estimation, and the prices that are used. According to Jun Sik Bae, North Korea's defense burden has grown steadily starting from the early 1970s, peaked in the mid 1990s, and then fell to 14–17 percent of GDP in the late 1990s. See Bae (2003)

[4] See the definition and discussion of economic rents in Chapter Three, pp. 14–15.

[5] See Wolf et al. (1983).

Paradoxes

The North Korean system is not only shrouded in obscurity, it is also immersed in paradoxes. The political philosophy proclaimed by the "Great Leader," Kim Il Sung, to guide the state from its inception, and reiterated frequently since then by Kim Jong Il and the North Korean media is that of *juche*. Ostensibly, *juche* exalts self-reliance and the independence of the North Korean state and its leadership from the influence of other states and other external forces. The paradox is that, unlike the autarchic economic course endorsed and actually pursued by the Soviet state, North Korea's "self-reliance" has meant its perennial reliance on wealth transfers from abroad in almost all the 55 years of its existence.[6] This is reflected (although probably understated) by annual current account deficits between 3 percent and 7 percent of North Korea's GDP throughout this period.[7]

The file of paradoxes is replete. Another one is the sharp antinomy between North Korean self-characterization as a "socialist paradise" at the same time as it pursues and persecutes anyone who tries to escape. It reported a bumper crop in 2001, but famine conditions were acknowledged in 2002.[8] In the midst of pervasive national poverty, military spending continues to be large and is perhaps increasing, focusing not only on force maintenance but also on development of weapons of mass destruction.

---

[6] Nicholas Eberstadt whimsically observes that this paradox can be resolved by an elastic interpretation of *juche sasang* ("juche thought"). Extraction or extortion of wealth transfers from abroad is rendered compatible with "self-reliance" by interpreting it as resulting from the exercise of North Korea's power to garner tribute, thereby assuring its survival. See Eberstadt (2002). See also Eberstadt (1996). Eberstadt points out that the North Korean regime defines itself in antithesis to the old Yi Dynasty, which was locked into tributary relations with the "central power" of China. By the *juche* doctrine, North Korea is now the central power, so others should pay tribute to it.

[7] See Figure 3.1, Chapter Three, p. 16.

[8] A recent study explains the decline in crop production and the lack of investment in the agricultural sector while acknowledging unfavorable weather conditions in the 1990s. According to this report, the crop production of 2002 was about 3.84 million tons, which is about 2–2.5 million tons less than the estimated need of 6–6.5 million tons. About half of this shortage (more than 1 million tons) was filled through international food aid. See Korea Institute for International Economic Policy (2003).

To be sure, some of these paradoxes can be attributed to a combination of apocryphal data and deceptive propaganda from the North Korean state. Yet the bottom line remains: The North Korean system is baffling because of the obscurities and paradoxes in which it abounds.

CHAPTER THREE

Size, Growth, and Structure of the North Korean Economy

Data Problems

Estimates of North Korea's Gross Domestic Product or Gross National Income[1] vary widely for many reasons. They include the absence of reliable data for many components of the national accounts,[2] secrecy surrounding data that may be available internally but are not available externally, and a possible temptation by some analysts to invent data in the process of trying to make the best of the bad data that are available.[3]

Another problem associated with North Korean data stems from the legacy of Soviet accounting practices, which excluded "intermediate services" (for example, transportation, housing, health care, and

---

[1] Gross National Income (GNI) is gross domestic product (GDP) plus net income from abroad. For most countries, this addition (or subtraction if the economy is a net transmitter of income abroad) consists of earnings from assets held abroad (or earnings made by foreigners from assets held in the domestic economy). In North Korea's case, GNI typically exceeds GDP by the recurring, unrequited transfers from abroad (see Figure 3.1 and discussion on p. 16–18 below), including cash remittances from Koreans living abroad.

[2] The situation recalls Wolfgang Stolper's book *Planning Without Facts: Lessons in Resource Allocation from Nigeria's Development* (1966), which refers to Africa but is no less applicable to North Korea.

[3] Most of the data used in this report come from South Korea's National Statistical Office (KNSO) and the Bank of Korea.

education), from national accounts data. To the extent that this practice is replicated in North Korea's accounts, the result is underestimation of the economy's size. This source of underestimation is probably more than offset by another anomaly in North Korea as with other communist economic systems—namely, the tendency to generate negative "value added" in processing material inputs. That is, the market value of the final output may be less than the value of the inputs used in producing it, resulting in hidden inflation and deteriorated quality, especially of consumer goods.[4]

The North Korean GDP

Estimates of the size of the North Korean economy are usually scaled to data on the South Korean GDP (see Table 3.1). South Korea's Statistical Office estimated South Korea's GDP as 22 times that of the North in 1995, and between 25 and 27 times that of the North in the period from 1996 to 2002.[5] Other estimates have scaled South Korea's GDP as high as 40 times or even 50 times that of the North.[6] In the simulations to be discussed later, we vary the relative size of North Korea's GDP between 3 percent, 4 percent, and 5 percent of that of South Korea.[7]

Table 3.2 summarizes estimates made by the South Korean National Security Office of comparative rates of growth in North and South Korea during the 1990–2002 period.

---

[4] See Rowen and Wolf (1990), pp. 2–4, 22–24, 68–69, ff.

[5] See Korea National Statistics Office (2002), pp. 13–14.

[6] The estimate of 40 times is from the Cato Institute in Washington, D.C. The estimate of 50 times is from Ambassador Lee In-Ho, President of the Korea Foundation in private conversation with the author at UCLA, February 2003.

[7] See Chapter Five, p. 34, and the appendix, pp. 63–64.

Table 3.1
North Korean and South Korean Gross Domestic Products, 2002
(in North and South Korean won and U.S. dollars)[8]

	North Korea			South Korea		
	Won	U.S. dollars		Won	U.S. dollars	
		Nominal exchange rates	PPP[a] rates		Nominal exchange rates	PPP rates
Size of economy (GDP) (billions)	21,331	17.0	22.8[b]	596,881	476.7	727.8
Per capita national product	952	759	1018	12,673	10,012	15,542[b]

SOURCES: Bank of Korea; World Bank; Economist (2004).
[a] PPP = purchasing power parity.
[b] Authors' calculations from Economist (2004). South Korea's population is 47.1 million, that of North Korea approximately 22.4 million (Economist, 2004). All of the figures for North Korea should be regarded as rough approximations with a wide band of uncertainty attached to them.

The nearly 12 percent reversal shown in Table 3.2 in South Korea's growth between 1997 and 1998 (from +5 percent to –6.7 percent), reflects the East Asian financial crisis of that period. It is difficult to explain and reconcile North Korea's reported (and perhaps bogus) high growth and bumper crops in 1999 with famine and acute poverty in 2000.

---

[8] All of the figures for North Korea should be regarded as rough approximations with a wide band of uncertainty attached to them. During Kim Jong Il's extended train trip from Pyongyang to Moscow in 2002 Kim was quoted by his accompanying Russian interlocutor as having observed that "many countries exaggerate their disasters to get more aid from the global community" (see Breen, 2002, p. 6). Although Kim's observation was reportedly made about poverty in Africa rather than in North Korea, it is worth bearing in mind in interpreting and evaluating the North Korean data shown in Table 3.1.

Table 3.2
North and South Korean GDP Growth Rates,
1990–2002 (in percentage per year)

Years	North Korea	South Korea
1990	−3.7	9.0
1991	−3.5	9.2
1992	−6.0	5.4
1993	−4.2	5.5
1994	−2.1	8.3
1995	−4.1	8.9
q1996	−3.6	6.8
1997	−6.3	5.0
1998	−1.1	−6.7
1999	6.2	10.9
2000	1.3	9.3
2001	3.7	3.1
2002	1.2	6.3
Cumulative growth, 1990–2002	−22.2	81.0
Average GDP growth rate, 1990–2002, %/yr	−1.7	6.2

SOURCES: Bank of Korea; Korean Ministry of Unification (cited in Oh and Hassig, 2000, p. 42); and authors'
calculations.

Structural Characteristics of North Korea's Economy

North Korea's economy has been described in terms of three sectors:
the primary sector, comprising agriculture (employing about 40 percent of the population), mining, and state factories; the defense sector; and the "court economy," which provides goods and services for
North Korea's elites and largely functions apart from the rest of the
economy.[9] The court economy has been characterized as "able to se-

---

[9] See Oh and Hassig (2000), pp. 65–67. The estimate of the farm population is from the
Korean National Statistical Office.

cure state resources but unaccountable to the economic bureaucracy."[10]

From the standpoint of North Korea's limited economic relations with the outside world, this court economy is an aspect of what can be described technically as a rent-seeking economic system. The rents realized by and for North Korea's political, military, and technical elites provide resources crucial for the leadership's maintenance of control and loyalty of the approximately 3 million beneficiaries at the top, and for perpetuation of the system.[11]

A central part of the economy's structure is its overdeveloped military sector. This includes the million-plus armed forces, defense research and development of nuclear and other weapons of mass destruction,[12] and industrial production of conventional and unconventional weapons. In relation to the size of its population, North Korea's armed forces are the largest in Asia. In both respects—military production and military forces—overdevelopment of the military sector emulates North Korea's Soviet antecedent while exceeding the latter in relative terms.

Taken together, reported budgetary military spending and production by military industry (to the extent the latter is not already included in budgeted military spending) represent between 25 percent and over 30 percent of North Korea's GDP,[13] a range reflecting the uncertainties of the estimate. The actual size of the military sector as a share of the North Korean economy is probably closer to the upper end of this range because of what is not included in the data on which the estimates are based. For example, unrequited capital transfers and other rents extracted from other countries probably redound

---

[10] Oh and Hassig (2000), p. 66.

[11] In economic terminology, rents are quasi-monopoly earnings, or super-normal profits that, in a competitive market environment, are usually short-lived. See discussion below, pp. 14–15.

[12] Ample recourse to Pakistan's Abdul Qadeer Khan has presumably enabled North Korea to economize on its costs of acquiring the technology for its nuclear weapons and delivery programs. See Hersh (2003).

[13] cf. Wolf et al. (1989, 1995).

in considerable measure to the benefit of the military sector. Furthermore, priorities in resource allocation to the military and preferential treatment of its leadership and personnel are not reflected in these estimates of the military share of GDP, just as they were not adequately reflected in Soviet practices of bygone days.

Another way of expressing the military's dominance in the North Korean economy is by comparing military outlays per active military personnel with nonmilitary outlays per nonmilitary persons in all of North Korea. Military spending per active North Korean military personnel is between $3,900 and $5,500, depending on whether the dollar conversions are made at nominal foreign exchange rates or purchasing power parity rates, respectively. The corresponding range for nonmilitary national product per nonmilitary personnel is between $509 and $707. Although military outlays in other countries are typically capital intensive, the 8:1 ratio between per-capita outlays for the military and nonmilitary population in North Korea is extraordinarily high: For the United States the roughly comparable figure is about 5:1.

One characteristic of North Korea's economy is unique. This is what we have labeled North Korea's "rent-seeking" economic system.[14] This means that the North Korean system is focused and relies on extracting some form of quasi-monopoly profits (i.e., rents) from its dealings with the rest of the world.

Rent-seeking behavior refers not only to the use of productive resources to extracting rents but also to the deliberate use of declaratory policies, threats, and negotiatory stances by the government to acquire such rents. In the North Korean context, rent-seeking behavior also encompasses "protective services" extended in the form of promises to refrain from aggressive actions—such as development of nuclear weapons, missile delivery systems, and other weapons of mass destruction—in exchange for payments, whether through foreign aid in currency or in kind, as fuel or food, as loans understood as unlikely

---

[14] See Krueger (1974); Buchanan, Tollison, and Tullock (eds.) (1980).

to be repaid, or as resources provided under the 1994 Framework agreement to North Korea by "protected" signatories.[15]

To be sure, rent-seeking by governments other than North Korea's as well as by private, commercial firms is not unprecedented. Governments and other public agencies have often sought and sometimes acquired special concessions enabling them to realize monopoly rents from subsequent transactions. Governments and companies have sometimes acquired exclusive licenses or other privileges allowing them to explore and develop oil deposits or to engage in exclusive sales or purchase agreements from which rents have been realized. Consider, for example, Iraq's former extraction of subventions from Saudi Arabia in return for Iraqi abstention from aggression against Saudi Arabia; the Soviet Union's extraction of concessions from Finland in return for retention by that country of its sovereignty prior to World War II; Wal-Mart's monopsonistic exactions from multiple small-scale suppliers; and pharmaceutical companies' use of patents and other legal devices to recoup (and thereby motivate) the huge prior research and development (R&D) outlays incurred in developing therapeutic drugs. However, such rents and the special arrangements on which they depend are usually only temporary because they are redressed by disclosure and, sooner or later, by the normal operation of competitive market forces or, failing this corrective process, by antitrust regulatory policies.

What is different and unique about North Korea's rent-seeking is that it focuses on specific activities insulated from normal market competition because the activities themselves are formally illegal but enforcement of the laws is lax. These are the circumstances surrounding North Korea's exports of drugs, counterfeit currencies, and various categories of weapons including missiles and, prospectively, nuclear weapons technology. North Korea's rent-seeking has perennially followed a pattern of finding and exploiting these off-limits, extra-market niches.

---

[15] See below, p. 18.

As noted earlier, the North Korean state has been dependent since its inception on unrequited wealth transfers through humanitarian and other grants and aid from abroad and extra-legal rents derived from illicit exports.

In the half century of its existence, North Korea has perennially incurred current-account deficits. In almost every year since its formation, its imports have exceeded its exports, without recorded capital imports equivalent to this gap. Figure 3.1 shows the annual trade deficits on North Korea's current account from 1960 to 2001.

The figures shown in the "trade deficits" line probably underestimate North Korea's actual current account deficits, among other reasons because some of its imports typically were accompanied by substantial but unrecorded imports of associated services. The data in Figure 3.1 also exclude weapons imports before 1990 from the Soviet

Figure 3.1—North Korea's Imports, Exports, and Trade Deficits, 1960–2001 (in millions of U.S. dollars)

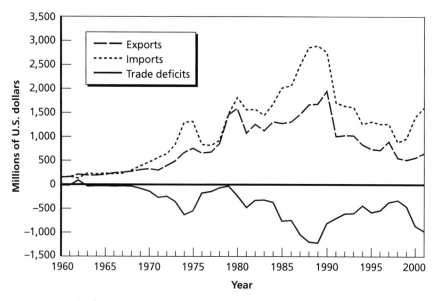

SOURCES: Bank of Korea; Korean Ministry of Unification; United Nations World Food Programme; Hwang (1993); Flake (1998); Eberstadt (1996); Noland (1996).

Union and thereafter from other sources. Nor do the Figure 3.1 data allow for barter transactions that may have ensued between North Korea and Pakistan involving exchange of missile delivery vehicles and technology from North Korea for uranium enrichment technology and other nuclear equipment and technology from Pakistan.

Estimates of North Korea's implicit foreign debt are based on the magnitude of the accumulated annual trade deficits.[16] North Korea does not recognize these debts. Instead, the accumulated current account deficits are construed by North Korea to represent capital transfers provided by its various benefactors for reasons of their own: for example, by the Soviet Union from 1960 to 1990 to support its ideological partner, and by China over the past dozen years for both this ideological reason and also to forestall a flow of refugees from North Korea that China feared would ensue if poverty in North Korea were to become more acute as a result of curtailed imports from China.

In 1990, trade between the former Soviet Union and North Korea was about $2.3 billion (more than one half of North Korea's foreign trade), but in the 1990s North Korea's trade with Russia declined sharply to an annual level of $100 million. This was partly the result of tensions between the two countries over the non-redemption of North Korea's debts to Russia. Thereafter China became North Korea's largest trading partner as well as its largest donor of aid. Currently, China accounts for about one-third of North Korea's foreign trade with recorded bilateral annual trade of more than $700 million. China's major exports to North Korea include crude oil, corn, and rice, all of which are priced below world market prices; hence, the actual value of this trade is significantly higher than its recorded value.[17]

---

[16] See estimates of North Korea's foreign debt, 1985–1998, in Oh and Hassig (2000), p. 46. More recent estimates by Kamil Akramov based on South Korean sources have placed North Korea's external debt at $12–12.5 billion, although North Korea stalwartly disavows any such obligation.

[17] Korea Institute for International Economic Policy (2003).

In the past decade, Russia has virtually ceased to be a source of wealth transfers to North Korea whereas China continues to provide them in large amounts. The forgone Russian sources were superseded by transfers from Japan, South Korea, and the United States from 1994 until 2000 under the so-called Framework agreement. The Framework, terminated in 2001, provided oil, food, and light-water reactors from the three countries (with the European Union a subsequent contributor) in exchange for a commitment by North Korea to end its nuclear weapons program and cultivate relations with South Korea.

In addition to its exports of metallic ores and other commodities and its perennial receipt of unrequited capital transfers, North Korea has other means of acquiring external resources. These other revenue sources include various nominally proscribed exports of drugs; counterfeit currencies; missile technology to Pakistan, Iran, and probably other states; and perhaps nuclear weapons technology to Iran. Some of these receipts are included in the export data shown in Figure 3.1. North Korea's hard-currency receipts from these sources have been variously estimated between $0.5 billion and $1.0 billion annually over the period from 1990 to 2002. Much of the revenues derived from illegal transactions are believed to be excluded from North Korea's budgetary processes, and are presumed to accrue in large measure directly to Kim Jong Il in the form of segregated, personal accounts.[18]

Unrequited capital transfers, unreported extra-legal exports, and the economic rents that accrue from them are crucial elements of the North Korean economic "system." They provide centrally controlled resources whose disposition by Kim Jong Il ensures the fealty and support of the limited numbers of civilian and military elite among the bureaucracy, the technocracy, and the military establishment at the top of the system's pyramid.[19] In turn, these elites exercise pervasive control over the mass of the North Korean population through a

---

[18] See Eberstadt (1996); Solomon and Choi (2003); and Oh and Hassig (2000), pp. 65–67.

[19] See Oh and Hassig (2000), p. 42.

combination of repression, fear, and occasional benefactions. These instruments of control may be jeopardized but can probably be maintained notwithstanding protracted negative or stagnant economic growth and periodic famines. This bleak prognosis is based on the fact that the external resources acquired by the central leadership and through which it exercises control are largely unaffected—and perhaps might even be increased—by internal economic setbacks in North Korea.

CHAPTER FOUR

How the System Might Unravel: Scenarios for Reunification

Diminished Attention to Reunification

The political prospects for Korean reunification and for the unraveling of the North Korean system have fluctuated intermittently over the past dozen years. Following the demise of Kim Il Sung in 1994, foreign observers periodically conjectured that the regime's survival might be imperiled. Circumstances contributing to these conjectures have included the apparently serious deterioration in the North Korean economy, as well as the gradual, uncertain, and usually obscure process by which Kim Jong Il has acquired most of the power possessed by his father.

In recent years, these conjectures have receded for two reasons:

- The North Korean regime's demonstration of its durability, especially its undiminished ability to maintain one of the dozen largest conventional military establishments in the world. Notwithstanding serious economic adversities, North Korea's durability seems to belie the credibility of scenarios envisaging the system's unraveling.
- The focus of external attention has shifted away from conjectures about unraveling and reunification, concentrating instead on more immediate concerns: specifically, North Korea's re-

peated announcements and threats that it would reprocess spent nuclear fuel rods and/or enrich natural uranium to produce nuclear weapons, or that it has already done so and might do more of the same unless its demands for security guarantees coupled with economic benefits were met.

In prior years, when serious consideration was given to the possibility that the regime might collapse and reunification might impend, observers were surprised when this did not occur. Currently, when relatively little attention is focused on possible reunification, we might be surprised once again—but this time in the reverse direction. The possibility of reunification might become relevant and timely as well as unexpected.

Three Reunification Scenarios[1]

Several scenarios are briefly sketched below to illustrate some plausible circumstances under which the North Korean regime might be replaced or absorbed and reunification of the Korean peninsula might be accomplished. The scenarios provide a backdrop for estimating a range of costs with which reunification would then be associated. We will turn to these cost estimates in Chapter Five.

Scenario A: Unification Through System Evolution and Integration

North Korea might adopt and implement (perhaps at an accelerated pace) China's remarkably successful economic model: liberalizing the economic system, opening trade and capital transactions, decreasing centralized economic control, and increasing decentralization and

---

[1] The following discussion draws heavily on prior RAND work, especially, Pollack and Lee (1999) and unpublished work by Bruce W. Bennett and Jennifer Lind on transitioning to Korean unification—implications for U.S. and ROK force requirements. Although our discussion draws on this prior work, we make various judgments and describe illustrations that condense and depart from the previously cited RAND studies in important respects.

marketization of economic activity.[2] Under these circumstances, the economic system in the North would become more compatible with that in the South. The process could be likened to the experience of China and Taiwan. In fact, not only have the economies of the mainland and of Taiwan expanded their trade and investment trans-actions several-fold in recent years, but the structures of the two economies are becoming more compatible, although certainly not identical.[3]

Under these circumstances, some form of political federalism be-tween North and South Korea might be envisaged, including closer contacts between the two military establishments, joint training and military exercises between them, and denuclearization of the North.

To be sure, developments along these lines would take several years to emerge. Moreover, they would probably ensue only under the most favorable and perhaps less plausible circumstances. Some recent evidence, while mildly encouraging, is still far less than would make this scenario appear probable rather than only conceivable.[4]

Scenario B: Unification Through Collapse and Absorption[5]

As discussed earlier, the North Korean regime has shown an extraor-dinary capacity to withstand severe internal economic adversity. In large part this capacity has been due to the regime's dexterity and ef-fectiveness in acquiring economic rents and other sources of support from outside sources. These resources have been deployed to main-tain and strengthen the regime's centralized political control, not-

---

[2] Evidence of movement in these directions has been periodically reported by and, more recently, has been observed in Pyongyang. See, for example, "Through a Glass Darkly," 2004. While the earlier reports were not sustained, the more recent ones may be.

[3] As one indicator, China's ownership of investments in fixed assets in 2002 was 43 percent by government, 15 percent by individuals, and the remaining 42 percent by collectives and others (*China Statistical Yearbook*, 2003, p. 187). Roughly comparable figures for Taiwan are 23 percent government, 13 percent individuals and partnerships, and 62 percent private companies (General Report (Taiwan Statistical Tables) 1. General Condition of Enterprise Units of All Industry, 2001, http://eng.dgbas.gov.tw/mp.asp?mp=2).

[4] See "Through a Glass Darkly."

[5] See Pollack and Lee (1999), pp. 57–66.

withstanding the presumptively disruptive effects of famine, decimation of the North Korean populace, and any emergent signs of internal resistance. But what has been true in the past might not be replicable in the future.

Were North Korean economy to experience further severe setbacks, and were they to be accompanied by North Korea's inability to acquire sufficient external resources to sustain its large military establishment and its supporting defense industry, the ensuing situation might differ from that of the past. If the economic adversity were severe and external subventions were limited, the regime might be unable to support its military assets and to maintain order and control in the separate regions of North Korea. Divisions might emerge within the party leadership, and the preeminence of Kim Jong Il might be compromised. If contacts and communication between the military establishments in the North and the South had previously occurred, such contacts might be expanded, leading to some form of comity and cooperation between the North and Korean military establishments. With appropriate financial inducements, this in turn might lead to the demilitarization and denuclearization of the North, and absorption of the North Korean regime into that of the South.[6] Of course, this trajectory is not the only one that might ensue following "collapse." Instead, the ensuing circumstances might entail the emergence of regional warlords and conflict among them— circumstances that might then link with a scenario of unification through conflict.

Scenario C: Unification Through Conflict

Conflict between North and South Korea might arise from any of several possible precipitating events: for example, North Korean invasion of the South based on a real or fancied provocation from the South; a North Korean interpretation of a provocation from the United States as one in which South Korea is closely complicit; inter-

---

[6] To be sure, there is a jump if not a leap from the circumstances summarized in this scenario, and the posited outcome. Plausible intervening steps are described in unpublished RAND work by Bennett and Lind.

nal conflict within North Korea spilling over into the South; or by "preventive" intervention into North Korea from the South to forestall such a spillover or to forestall other possibly threatening circumstances in the North. In any of these circumstances, it is plausible that the United States and China would cooperate—either tacitly or overtly—to end the conflict by having their respective military forces intervene to restore and preserve order and especially to prevent further escalation, particularly if some casualties had been incurred on either or both sides.[7] It is also likely that the conflict would have inflicted considerable damage on South Korea's capital stock, which would raise reconstruction costs in the South rather than direct capital costs of reunification in the North.

If a conflict scenario were to include within it insurgency in North Korea, the burden of achieving sufficient security for reunification to proceed would be heavier, and the attendant costs would rise accordingly. Assuming sufficient cooperation between the United States and China to reestablish order and enforce the peace, unification of the peninsula might be accomplished within a few years, perhaps based on some form of federalism between North and South. We assume that the central government of such a reunified Korea would adopt institutions similar to or congruent with those currently in place in the South. As part of a U.S.-China cooperative agreement, these developments might plausibly be accompanied by conditional agreements to substantially reduce if not remove U.S. forces from the Korean peninsula.

---

[7] In this study, we do not consider the unlikely possibility that efforts to prevent escalation might fail and that weapons of mass destruction might be utilized instead. One reason we deem this possibility to be unlikely is that both the United States and China would be strongly motivated to use their diplomatic and military leverage to prevent it. Another reason is that the ramifications of such an escalatory scenario would carry us far afield from the intended focus of our study.

CHAPTER FIVE

The Capital Costs of Korean Reunification: Estimation and Management

Fluctuating Interest in Reunification

As previously noted, the political prospect of Korean unification has frequently surfaced over the past two decades, preceding the demise of Kim Il Sung in 1994 and especially in the decade since then. For decisionmakers in Seoul and Western policymakers, that prospect has frequently been sidelined by external events that have diverted attention away from Korean reunification. These distractions have included—besides those mentioned earlier—the protracted and costly process of German reunification since 1991, the financial crisis in Korea and Southeast Asia in 1997 and 1998, and North Korea's brandishing of nuclear weapons or periodic claims to have programs under way to provide them in the early 1990s and especially since 2003.

Reluctance to focus attention on reunification has been reinforced by estimates that the associated costs may be enormous. Depending on varying assumptions and scenarios, these costs have been estimated as spanning a range between several hundred billion and several trillion dollars.[1] This huge range reflects both a diversity of

---

[1] See Noland, Robinson, and Liu (1998); and Noland (2000). Chapter Six presents a brief overview of the differing methods and results of prior cost estimates by several institutions and analysts in Korea and the United States.

assumptions and a plethora of uncertainties including ignorance about the real economic conditions in North Korea, the circumstance and timing of possible reunification scenarios, and the appropriate economic and other goals that reunification should seek. Because the estimates of Korean reunification costs have been so high, all of the relevant "players" who would be affected by these costs—especially South Korea but also the United States, Japan, China, and the international financial institutions—have been inclined toward an attitude of "not on my watch" and "let's wait and see."

Apart from the enormous political and social problems that Korean reunification would confront, it is generally and plausibly presumed that reunification would impose even larger relative cost burdens on South Korea and its allies than the substantial costs that have materialized (and indeed are still accumulating) in Germany's reunification. From 1991 through 2004, $1.4 trillion of West Germany's wealth was transferred to the East, representing about 5–6 percent of Germany's cumulative GDP during this period.[2] Relative income levels are much lower and the relative populations are much larger in the North Korean-South Korean case than in the East German-West German case. Per capita GDP in North Korea relative to South Korea is much lower (perhaps 8 percent or less) than the 20-30 percent proportion between East Germany and West Germany in 1990.[3] North Korea's population is about one-half that of South Korea whereas the East German population was only one-quarter that of West Germany. Thus, because the relative income gaps and the relative populations are larger in Korea than in Germany, it has been inferred that the resulting cost burden would be relatively higher for Korean reunification than German reunification.

---

[2] Solomon and Choi, 2003; authors' calculation.

[3] Prior to German reunification, U.S. government estimates had erroneously placed East German per capita GDP over 80 percent that of West Germany. After reunification it appeared that these estimates were wide of the mark by a factor of 3 or 4; East German per capita GDP was about one-fourth (or less) that of West Germany. See CIA (1999).

However, several countervailing considerations might reduce the relative costs of Korean reunification and make them less forbiddingly high and gloomy than the foregoing story implies.

- The economic burden on North Korea from its huge military establishment is much greater in relative terms than was the corresponding burden of East Germany's military establishment preceding German reunification. As previously noted, in North Korea the military establishment absorbs 20 to 30 percent or more of the North Korean GDP.
- In contrast, in East Germany in 1990–1991 the Soviet Union was the predominant military establishment. Although Soviet forces imposed some burden on the East German economy, most of their costs were borne by the Soviet Union.
- Reunification in Korea may provide an opportunity for realizing appreciable resource savings by linking the *building-down* of North Korea's military to the *building-up* of its relatively small and deprived civilian capital base.
- Finally, it is probably true that prevailing attitudes among the North Korean population as well as the impediments imposed by Korea's physical geography would conduce to more limited population movement from North to South than that which preceded and accompanied German reunification after the wall between East and West Germany came down. The unfolding and anticipated surge of East Germans toward the West imposed a greater urgency on relieving the disparities between West and East German per capita income than might ensue in the event of Korean reunification.

Simulation and Uncertainties

That there are profound and pervasive uncertainties surrounding estimation of reunification costs hardly needs mentioning yet is so important as to require it. Many of these uncertainties are reflected or implied in the brief descriptions of the three reunification scenarios in

Chapter Four. To simplify our estimates, we focus on the capital costs of rapidly doubling North Korean GDP, acknowledging that even these costs are profoundly uncertain.

In addition, unification would entail such other costs as those relating to humanitarian efforts, economic stabilization, regime replacement, political reeducation, job training, administration and bureaucratic overhaul, and social integration. These broader costs are even more uncertain than the capital costs, and could exceed the capital costs. Even so, substantial disparities in economic and social conditions between the Northern and Southern parts of Korea would still remain, disparities that a unified government would have to manage carefully to assure reasonable stability in the North.

Still, it can be argued that management and containment of those broader costs should be viewed as tasks that typically are discharged by many governments in the course of their normal although pressing obligations and functions. Indeed, there are many instances of countries and governments which function with tolerable effectiveness and stability notwithstanding deep political, social, cultural, and economic disparities and rifts within them. Examples include Indonesia (e.g., Christian Ambonese and Muslim Javanese), Belgium (the Flemish and Walloons), East and West Ukraine, Italy (the Mezzogiorno and the more prosperous Piemonte region), not to mention the United States (e.g., California and Mississippi), and even within New York City (including the boroughs of Manhattan and Queens). In sum, countries can be unified while often remaining far from uniformity or homogeneity.

The Model

The simulation model we apply is described in the appendix; it is based on five key assumptions:

1. Achieving a doubling of North Korea's GDP and per capita GDP in a relatively short period would constitute a sufficiently large economic boost to enable the unified state to proceed and to manage its affairs in the more or less normal, although admittedly imperfect manner, in which other new states and govern-

ments typically manage their internal problems.[4] (Doubling North Korea's GDP in four or five years implies a GDP growth rate between 14 percent and 18 percent annually; the implied six-year doubling rate would be 12 percent annual growth. These rates are unusual but not entirely unprecedented.)

2. The rapid economic growth implied by the previous assumption, combined with the pattern of institutional reform implied by the fifth assumption below, will contribute to a manageably low rate of population exodus from North Korea.

3. The core capital costs of doubling North Korean GDP can be estimated as the incremental capital requirements for reaching the objective of doubling GDP in the North.

4. The net capital costs can be lowered modestly by military savings realized from lowering military spending below its extremely high current levels in North Korea and, to a considerably lesser extent, in South Korea.

5. The capital costs of unification will be higher or lower depending on the pace and effectiveness of what we refer to as *institutional reform*.[5]

Each of these assumptions is arguable, as is the structure of the model described in the appendix. With respect to the model, we believe its simplicity is an advantage rather than a shortcoming. In general, it is desirable that models be no more refined and demanding than is consistent with the quality and extent of the data available for implementing them. For North Korea, the requisite data are distinctly limited.

Our estimates of reunification costs are not specifically or directly tied to any one of the three scenarios. Instead, variations in the key parameters used in the simulations are intended to reflect differences among the scenarios, as well as the uncertainties embedded in

---

[4] See further discussion of this point, pp. 46–47. The GDP to be doubled according to this target would be the GDP level prevailing under one or another of the unification scenarios.

[5] See discussion below, pp. 36–37.

them. For example, the range of incremental capital-output ratios (ICORs)—varying from 3 to 5—used in the simulations can be associated, respectively, with scenario A (unification through evolution and integration), scenario B (collapse and absorption), and scenario C (conflict).[6] A higher ICOR, implying larger capital costs of reunification, is likely to be associated with a more conflicted reunification process—hence, with scenario C rather than scenario A.[7]

Comparing ICOR values among countries is suggestive although not determinative because of the numerous factors that will influence the coefficient in different contexts, including resource endowments, capital intensities of different industries, prevailing regulatory constraints, and management capabilities.

Table 5.1 shows a range of ICOR values between 2.7 and 5.1 for China, Japan, South Korea, and Taiwan during periods when they were experiencing rapid economic growth.[8]

In all the scenarios and simulations our estimates relate to the capital requirements associated with meeting the stipulated aggregate

---

[6] The *Incremental Capital-Output Ratio* (ICOR) is the ratio of new investment to additional output. The ICOR for a given country measures the increase in output resulting from a unit increase in the country's total capital stock. The inverse of the ICOR is thus an upper-bound estimate of the average marginal product of capital for the macroeconomy. In general, the lower the ICOR, the more efficiently new investment is employed. An economy's ICOR includes the cost of both infrastructure and industrial capital. For example, the costs of rehabilitating North Korea's electricity grid network—which has been estimated at $3–5 billion—would be a component of the North Korean ICOR. See Nautilus Institute (2000). See also Vanek and Studenmund (1968) and Gianaris (1970).

[7] Auty (ed.) (2001).

[8] In November 2004, in a conversation with one of the authors of the report, the Korean Development Institute's specialist in North Korea and unification issues expressed his view that North Korea's ICOR would initially be quite low—about 2 rather than 3—because unification would be accompanied by reduced regulatory restrictions on the efficient use of capital. Reducing these constraints would, he thought, sharply raise capital productivity resulting in a low ICOR. Later in the process, he opined, ICOR would rise to 3 but was unlikely to go much higher. While capital infusions could be highly productive, he believed limitations on North Korea's capacity to absorb capital would provide a cap on the appropriate magnitude of such infusions.

Table 5.1
Incremental Capital-Output Ratios (ICOR)
and GDP Growth in East Asian Countries

	GDP growth	ICOR
China		
1991–1995	11.6	3.4
1996–2000	8.4	4.5
2001–2003	8.0	5.1
Japan		
1961–1970	10.2	3.2
South Korea		
1981–1990	9.2	3.2
Taiwan		
1981–1990	8.0	2.7

SOURCE: Kwan (2004).

GDP growth target for the North.[9] We do not, for example, attempt to translate these capital cost estimates into the present value of consumption expenditures in the North that would be associated with realization of the annual growth rates posited in the simulations.

The three illustrative scenarios may also affect and be affected by the parameter relating to Institutional Reform Strategy (IRS)—embracing economic liberalization, property rights, and the rule of law. For example, scenario B may be associated with more rapid IRS, resulting in lower capital costs than A or C. We assign an arbitrary weight in the simulations for the IRS parameter ranging from 1 to 3, implying, respectively, that costs are as estimated from the other parameters in the simulation model or, alternatively, that these costs are doubled or tripled, reflecting slower or slowest implementation, respectively, of institutional reform. The rationale for varying the IRS multiple with respect to the pace of reform is that capital will be more or less efficiently allocated and utilized depending on whether the pace and effectiveness of institutional reform are rapid and high, or slow and low. With slow and limited market liberalization and the limited prevalence of the rule of law, capital will be

---

[9] See below, Chapter Five, Table 5.2, p. 39.

less efficiently utilized and the capital costs of reunification will thereby increase.

The following are some of the other major uncertainties reflected in the various parameters used in the simulations:

- North Korea has about 1.1 million men in its armed forces and about three or four times that number in its reserves, and a military spending share of GDP of 25–30 percent. South Korea's active military forces are about 680,000 with reserve forces several times that number, and its defense spending share is about 2.7–2.8 percent.[10] The essence of the idea mentioned earlier for managing and limiting the costs of reunification is to shrink the combined military forces of South and North Korea from over 1.7 million to perhaps 400,000, with the bulk of this reduction realized by decreasing North Korea's forces, and reallocating the resource savings to defray part of the capital build-up costs in the North. The assumed difference between preunification and postunification military spending in the North is reflected by different values assigned to the North's military spending parameter γ_i; the assumed difference between preunification military spending and postunification in the South is reflected by different values assigned to the South's military spending parameter β_i.
- The paucity and unreliability of data on North Korea's economy and the ratio between its GDP and South Korea's is reflected in the wide range of values assigned to this ratio, α_i (between .03 and .05), depending on whether North Korea's GDP is assumed to be 3 percent, 4 percent, or 5 percent of South Korea's GDP, corresponding to per capita product in the North approximately between 6 percent and 10 percent of that of South Korea.

---

[10] South Korea's defense spending was $11.4 billion and $13.3 billion in 2001 and 2002, respectively; its corresponding GDPs in those years were $422 billion and $476 billion. See IISS (2004). See also Wolf, Bamezai, et al. (2000) for similar estimates in both nominal exchange rates and purchasing power parity rates.

- The simulations further adopt a target, T_p, a goal of doubling North Korea's GDP in four or five years after unification. As mentioned above, we assume that this rapid rate of directly experienced economic progress would tend to limit population flows from North Korea to manageable levels and would provide a basis for sustained if slower growth thereafter. This crucial assumption differs from most other models, which typically have adopted goals of bridging or eliminating the difference between North-South per capita product. Adoption of the doubling target rather than the bridging one is based on two important though arguable judgments: first, that palpable, locally experienced changes (in this instance, progress and improved living conditions attendant to doubling of North Korea's GDP) are likely to have more influence on the reactions and behavior of North Korea's population than the more remote and impalpable level of living and income in the South; and second, that the engrained and conditioned insularity of the North's population may predispose them to avoid the risks of migrating to the South, and instead to prefer remaining in the North provided that conditions continued to improve.[11]

A third proposition supports the premise that population flows from North to South will be limited and can be manageable. This proposition reflects the basic economics underlying the widely differing living standards between North and South—namely, the difference in labor productivity between North and South (probably in the neighborhood of a tenfold difference), reflecting the enormously

---

[11] See below, pp. 52–54, where these two judgments are contrasted with the circumstances prevailing in Germany's reunification. Unpublished research by Kamil Akramov provides some support for these judgments. Nicholas Eberstadt has pointed out that South Korea's constitution confers the right to citizenship on the North Korean population. However, it does not follow that migration to the South should be presumed as a consequence of that right.

lower human capital endowment of the North Korean population.[12] Were North Korean labor to migrate to the South, the wage it could command in the South would reflect the substantially lower productivity of North Korean labor, *not* the higher labor productivity and higher consumption levels prevailing in the South. The drawing-power of South Korea's higher living standards will, as a result, be limited. And the experience of those who do migrate will tend to reinforce the fundamental economics of the situation.[13]

The appendix summarizes the simulation model, including the modest but nonetheless important role of resource savings from the military build-down in helping to meet the cost of building up North Korea's capital base and its labor productivity. The simulation model contains nine parameters, each of which acquires multiple values in separate runs of the model. The parameters are assigned varying values based partly on the data and analysis presented in previous chapters and partly on the authors' judgments about the range of uncertainties associated with each parameter and with the different scenarios described above.

Similarly, to reflect the uncertainties involved in estimating resource savings that can be derived from lowered levels of military spending postunification compared with preunification, we allow for a range of different values for the parameters corresponding to pre- and postunification military spending in the North and the South. Other parameters to which our simulation results are sensitive include the incremental capital-output ratio, which relates the investment requirements for raising output and income in postunification North Korea; and the institutional reform strategy, which encompasses the effectiveness with which marketization, property rights, and rule of

---

[12] Nicholas Eberstadt, in his comments on an earlier draft of this study, points out that seven-year-old children in North Korea were, according to a 1998 North Korean nutrition survey, 20 cm and 10 kg smaller than seven-year-olds in South Korea.

[13] Indeed, the disenchantment experienced by workers from the North who have actually migrated to the South can be attributed to this fundamental difference in labor productivity of North Korean labor, regardless of where it is located.

law can be established in the North or transferred from prevailing institutional structures in South Korea.

The IRS parameter also encompasses the possibility that the initial phase of unification might entail a form of governance in North Korea having some or many of the characteristics of a dependent territory. For example, responsibility for ensuring a reasonable degree of law and order might be exercised by South Korean military and paramilitary forces, with the attendant costs presumed to be reflected by the differing values assigned to the IRS parameter. A range of differing values is assigned to the IRS and other parameters in the model, reflecting—however imperfectly—the enormous uncertainties inevitably involved in the unification process.

As previously noted, a key assumption in the simulations is the setting of an aggregate target for economic progress in a postunified North Korea of doubling the North Korean GDP within a short three-, four-, or five-year period following reunification. This target implies annual growth rates of 24 percent, 18 percent, and 14 percent, respectively.[14]

Simulation Results

Estimating Korean reunification costs is, to borrow Winston Churchill's characterization of the Soviet Union, "A riddle wrapped in a mystery inside an enigma." Unification of the two Koreas—one a member of the Organization for Economic Cooperation and Development (OECD) with a per capita income over $10,000 and the other a "lights-out" but nuclear-capable dynastic state—is the riddle; how to link economic costs with a complex, multifaceted reunification process is the mystery; and North Korea's "dear leader" is the enigma.

We ran approximately 200 simulations using different combinations of the parameters whose respective ranges reflect the major uncertainties associated with each parameter. These uncertainties include the size of North Korea's preunification GDP relative to that of

---

[14] The ensuing discussion focuses on the four-year and five-year targets because the 24 percent growth rate is unrealistically high.

South Korea, the incremental capital formation required in the North to double its annual output in a short time, and the size of military resource outlays in the North compared to those in the South both before and after unification, and the circumstances (scenarios) attendant to the unification process.

In all of the simulations, we posit the same growth target—namely, doubling of North Korea's postunification GDP in either four or five years. This target implies an equivalent rate of growth in its per capita GDP on the premise that the North's population remains stable in the ensuing period compared to its actual decline in the recent past. If this ambitious goal can be achieved, it is not unreasonable, although surely debatable, to infer that population movement from North to South will be moderate and manageable.[15] Furthermore, we assume that a rapid doubling of GDP will install and propel a process of self-sustaining development in the North—an assumption that is both optimistic and debatable.

The capital costs of rapidly doubling North Korean GDP cover a range from $50 billion to nearly $670 billion (in 2003 U.S. dollars). If North Korea's initial GDP is as large as 8 percent of South Korea's, reunification costs will tend toward the higher end of this range; if the initial North Korean GDP is only 2 percent of that of South Korea, the corresponding capital requirements for doubling output in the postunification North will be reduced. If the incremental capital coefficient is as high as 5, reunification costs will be raised toward the higher end of the range. And if the preunification military spending share of North Korea's GDP is relatively higher but is substantially reduced after reunification, the savings from military build-down will be larger and the residual costs of reunification will be lowered. As noted earlier, reunification costs will vary inversely with whether the institutional reform strategy accompanying reunifi-

---

[15] From other research not separately reported here, it appears that the disposition of North Korea's population to move away from its home base may be more limited than in the German case. It may also be reasonable to assume that such population movement as occurs would be linked to family ties and support from family members in the South, thereby limiting the incremental costs of reunification.

cation is rapid, moderate, or slow. Net capital costs (after allowance for savings from military build-down) will also vary inversely if the target of doubling North Korean GDP is spread over five or six years rather than four.

Table 5.2 summarizes a selected range of parameter values and corresponding reunification costs referred to in the preceding discussion.

The assumptions and results summarized in Table 5.2 are based on a targeted doubling of North Korea's GDP in four years. If the targeted doubling time is extended to five years the estimated reunification costs (column 6 of Table 5.2) are reduced by $10–15 billion. The reduction is principally due to savings realized from the additional year of military build-down; the same investment requirements for commercial capital build-up are spread over five years, rather than four. Annual growth in the North's GDP shrinks to about 14 percent from the 18 percent required for doubling GDP in the four-year period. (The 14 percent growth rate is slightly below, while the 18 percent rate is above, growth rates experienced by China in the 1980s following its misguided "cultural revolution" in the late 1960s.)

Figures 5.1, 5.2, 5.3, and 5.4 show the sensitivity of the cost estimates to varying values of the parameters that indicate the relative

Table 5.2
Estimates of Reunification Costs: Selected Simulation Results (assuming four-year doubling of North Korean GDP)

(1) Pre-unification North/South GDPs	(2) Incremental Capital Coefficient	(3) Capital Build-Up Costs (billions of 2003 $)	(4) Military Build-Down Savings (billions of 2003 $)	(5) Institutional Reform Effectiveness (1–3)	(6) Reunification Costs (billions of 2003 $)
.03	3	86	36	1	50
.04	3	114	42	2	186
.05	4	191	49	3	524
.05	5	239	48	3	667

Figure 5.1
Sensitivity of Cost Estimates to North Korea's Preunification GDP
(subject to variations in Institutional Reform Strategy)

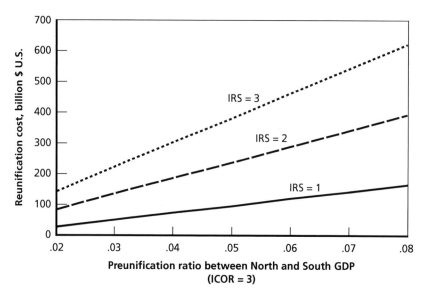

Figure 5.2
Sensitivity of Cost Estimates to Varying Incremental Capital Coefficients

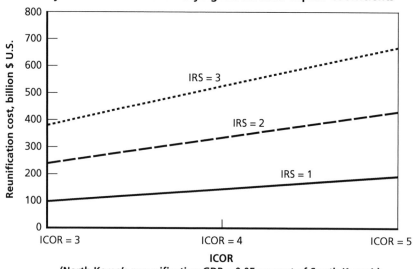

Figure 5.3
Sensitivity of Cost Estimates to Pace of Institutional Reform

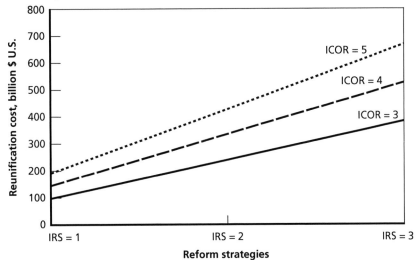

(North Korea's preunification GDP = 0.05 percent of South Korea's)

Figure 5.4
Sensitivity of Cost Estimates to Speed of Doubling North Korea's GDP

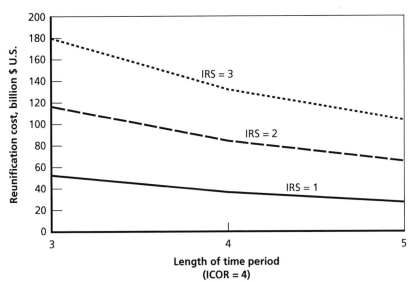

size of the preunification North Korean economy compared to that of the South, the size of the incremental capital coefficient, the institutional reform strategy accompanying reunification, and the resource savings from the North Korean military build-down. For mid-range values of the parameters, the resulting capital requirements estimate is between $330 and $350 billion.

Distributing the Costs of Korean Reunification

The simulations estimate aggregate capital costs over a four- or five-year period. It is reasonable to assume, or at least to hope, that realization of the ambitious doubling of the North Korean economy over this period would thereafter engender a process and a momentum for self-sustaining development in a reunified Korean economy.

How the total reunification costs might be distributed among various sources should be considered as well. Moreover, such burden-sharing could itself contribute to self-sustaining development. Reunification costs might be shared among four sources:

- private capital flows from South to North Korea (P_s)
- private capital flows from the rest of the world (P_r)
- public transfers from South Korea (T_s)
- public transfers from the rest of the world (T_r).

Rapid adoption of a sound institutional reform strategy would include encouragement of private, commercially motivated investment in the North. As noted above, the ingredients of a sound IRS include marketization of the economy, protection of property rights, and emergence of the rule of law in regulating transactions. Private resource flows from both South Korea (P_s) and the rest of the world (P_r) would be greater if IRS is rapid and effective. If private commercially motivated capital transfers were larger, the requisite need for public transfers—both from South Korea and the rest of the world—would be reduced.

Various ways of sharing the burden of capital costs might be devised.[16] If, for example, private and public capital transfers from South Korea bore, say, one-third of the total costs estimated in the simulations, the burden on the South's economy would span a range between $17 billion and $223 billion, representing between 0.9 percent and 9 percent, respectively, of South Korea's cumulative GDP over a four- to five-year period.[17] The remaining costs of reunification could plausibly be shared among private and public sources in the United States, Japan, China, the European Union, and the international financial institutions (World Bank, Asian Development Bank, etc.).

Although the assumption that two-thirds of the capital could come from sources outside Korea is arbitrary, it is plausible for several reasons. One reason is that the United States, China, and Japan share strong national interests in assuring a satisfactory transition process on the Korean peninsula. A second reason is that North Korea is a prospectively lucrative source of nonferrous metal ores for which China's rapidly growing economy has an enormous demand; capital investment from China and, to a lesser extent, from Japan are likely to result from this opportunity. A third reason is that South Korea's extensive and largely effective record of prior dealings with international financial institutions, combined with its relatively favorable rating in international capital markets, will tend to encourage capital flows from abroad.

To limit the cost burden placed on the South Korean government and other sources of public capital transfers, a promising insti-

---

[16] A study by the Hyundai Research Institute suggests that adoption of certain aspects of China's development experience (e.g., special economic zones located in coastal cities) might attract private direct investment in consignment manufacturing, electronics, garments, and transportation, and mining (for coal, lead, tungsten, zinc, copper, and other minerals in which North Korea is well-endowed). See Kim (2000). According to the Korean Trade Promotion Agency's survey, about 90 percent of South Korean firms in the mid-1990s had investment plans in the North (Jo, 1996).

[17] Assuming South Korea's cumulative GDP over four to five years is between $2.0 and $2.5 trillion. The mean of this range is comparable to the corresponding share of GDP represented by Germany's reunification costs. See below, p. 52.

tutional innovation might be integrated with the IRS. Demobilizing large elements of the North Korean military into a "civil construction corps" (CCC) could create a contract labor pool available for commercial and public employment by both commercial investors in North Korea and by the reunified Korean government. The CCC would entail two important benefits for Korean reconstruction. First, it could be a source of disciplined, relatively low-cost labor that, along with the other ingredients of IRS, could help attract private investment for the requisite capital build-up in the North. Second, the CCC could facilitate the transition of the North Korean military to civil employment, thereby reducing the risk of social instability if massive demobilization occurred without reasonable assurance of civil employment.[18]

---

[18] See Wolf (1999). The CCC idea initially was raised in conversations one of the authors had several years ago with a Korean official who, at the time, was a visiting scholar in the RAND Graduate School.

CHAPTER SIX

Other Estimates of Reunification Costs

Differing Sources and Types of Cost Estimates

The previous chapter described the wide range of estimates we have made using a simple estimating model and employing a limited number of parameters that reflect various assumptions and interactions relating to the reunification process. As noted above, these assumptions and parameters included the economic growth target stipulated for reunification, capital input requirements to reach the target, the accompanying pace and scale of military integration and downsizing, the scale of and constraints on population mobility, the pace of institutional reform, and opportunities for sharing the burden of reunification costs between public financing and commercially motivated private financing. As previously noted, our estimates of capital costs span a wide range that varies by a factor of 13 between the low and high estimates, depending on scenario combinations of these parameters. However, this range is narrower in dollars than estimates made by other institutions and analysts, and its absolute dollar magnitudes are substantially smaller.

These other estimates—probably no less fallible than our own—vary widely in the economic targets they adopt, the time horizons they cover, their baseline data assumptions, and the methodologies they employ. Consequently, they are not strictly comparable to our estimate or to one another, although each of them purports to measure something broadly and loosely termed "the costs of Korean reunification." Under this broad rubric, their variation extends from $290 billion made in 1994 and posited over a 32-year period to $3.2 trillion estimated in 1997 and extending over a ten-year period.

The Wide Range of Reunification Costs

Estimates of reunification costs have been made over the past decade by analysts at the Korean Development Institute (KDI), the Korean Institute for Economic Policy (KIEP), the Institute of International Economics in the United States, and by academic analysts at the Korean National University in Seoul. These studies used different methodologies, different unification dates, and different parameter assumptions in their computations. Most of the studies focus primarily on the capital costs of reunification, as does our own analysis, and do not encompass humanitarian, social, and psychological costs as well as other possible cost elements. However, apart from this similarity, the other studies and the cost estimates they have produced differ widely from our own. Virtually all of the other cost estimates assume that reunification must entail close convergence of income levels in the North and the South. By contrast, our study adopts a less ambitious and, we would opine, more realistic reunification goal of doubling per capita income in the North. Once this objective is achieved in four or five years, we further opine that the reunified Korean state is "on its way," so to speak, proceeding to work out its own destiny and its own parities and disparities between income levels and living standards in the North and the South.

There are, of course, other instances of countries in which significantly wide disparities in income levels and living styles have endured without undue jeopardy to stability. Italy's Mezzogiorno and the deep South in the U.S. provide two examples. Several western and central provinces in China—such as Hunan, Hubei, Anhui, and Xinjiang in comparison with the affluent coastal areas of Guandong,

Fujian, and Shanghai—are other examples. This is not to imply that these disparities are desirable or immutable. It is simply to suggest that the prevalence of wide income disparities between North and South Korea would be neither unprecedented nor incompatible with the experience of other states that have functioned in normal and stable ways while containing substantial internal disparities.

In any event, once the goal of doubling GDP has been reached in the North, we assume that subsequent capital flows between South and North, and between the rest of the world and the North, can proceed in the more or less familiar ways that such transactions typically occur in internal and international commerce.

In most of the other studies of Korean reunification, the implicit assumption is that the burden of meeting reunification costs would fall entirely on the South Korean economy rather than being shared among it and sources of support from other countries, international financial institutions, and between public institutions and private, commercially motivated businesses. While the methodologies used in the various studies differ (e.g., some of the models used Cobb-Douglas production functions, others use general equilibrium models or opportunity-cost models), they share the plausible premise that the later in time reunification occurs, the larger the costs of reunification. The reasoning behind this premise is that the gap between North and South Korea will widen over time. To the extent that the economic target posited for reunification requires a bridging of this gap, the inferred capital costs will rise because of the widening spread between per capita income in the South and the North. Underlying this premise is a view, shared by our own estimates as well, that reunification is a discrete event: The costs of unification begin when the reunification light goes on.

The KDI study distinguishes between "gradual" and "sudden" unification scenarios as well as varying income targets for reducing the South-North gap in the ensuing ten-year period. The resulting reunification cost estimates range between $360 billion and $1.13 trillion (in 1990 prices).

Another approach proceeds from the German unification experience and applies it to the prospective Korean case.[1] This study assumes that unification occurs over a five-year period, with complete "economic convergence" between the two Koreas occurring in 20 years. Its reunification cost estimates are $332 billion (in 1993 prices) during the first five years of the 20-year period.

Marcus Noland and associates developed a computable general equilibrium model to estimate reunification costs.[2] Using different reunification scenarios involving differing unification rates, differing capital-output coefficients, and different assumptions about labor migration from North to South, their estimates cover a range from $754 billion for a unification date of 1995 to $3.2 trillion for a unification date of 2000. According to their estimate, investment costs of Korean reunification are more sensitive to changes in the unification date than to changes in the capital coefficient; as noted earlier, the passage of time is presumed to widen the gap between the two Koreas, thereby raising reunification costs.

Table 6.1 summarizes these different studies.

----

[1] Bae (1996).

[2] Noland, Robinson, and Scatasta (1996).

Table 6.1
Other Estimates of Reunification Costs

Definition of Reunification Costs	Costs	Source
Incremental investment	$1.2 trillion–$2.4 trillion	Hwang (1993)
Total investment costs in 1990 prices over 10-year period	$360 billion–$1.13 trillion	Joon-Koo Lee (1995)
Present discounted value of capital transfers from South Korea to North Korea	$290 billion–$389 billion	Young Sun Lee (1994)
Additional fiscal burden on South Korea	$332 billion	Jin-Young Bae (1996)
Present discounted value of expenditures	$1.4 trillion–$3.2 trillion	Noland, Robinson, and Scatasta (1997)
Present discounted value of capital expenditures	$754 billion–$2.2 trillion	Noland, Robinson, and Scatasta (1996).
Transfers to North Korea from South Korea and other donors	0.25–5% of the South's GDP annually at the beginning; cumulative cost may vary from 55% to 190% of South's GDP over 20 years	Frecaut (2003)

NOTE: There are also other estimates of reunification costs. For example, Goldman-Sachs' estimate of reunification costs suggested that if unification were to occur in the near future, the cost might range from 0.77 to 1.2 trillion dollars over a decade. If reunification were to occur in 2010, the Goldman-Sachs cost estimates rise to $3.4–3.6 trillion over ten years (www.globalsecurity.org/military/ops/korea-crisis-intro.html).

CHAPTER SEVEN

Is Germany's Reunification Experience Relevant?

The apparent similarities between the reunification of West Germany (the Federal Republic of Germany, FRG) and East Germany and the possible reunification of South and North Korea are sufficient to warrant a brief review and recapitulation of the German experience to see what lessons might be extracted that would be relevant to the Korean case. However, the dissimilarities between the two cases are so prominent as to limit the relevance of the German reunification experience for possible future reunification in Korea.

The similarities include a common culture and language shared by the two Koreas and the two Germanys, the protracted political separation of the two parts (from 1945 to 1990 in the German case, and 1949 to the present in Korea), a centrally planned, regimented economic system in both East Germany and in North Korea, and a democratic, market-based system closely linked with the global economy in West Germany and in South Korea.

The dissimilarities between the two cases are at least equally prominent. East Germany's population was about one-fourth that of West Germany in 1990; North Korea's population is about one-half that of South Korea. East Germany's economy was about 8–9 percent of West Germany's; North Korea's economy is about 3–5 percent of South Korea's. Furthermore, the size of the military establishment and of the military economy supporting it was much smaller in East Germany (excluding the Soviet Union's military forces) than in North Korea. Also, the extent of contact, communication, and trade between East and West Germany prior to unification was vastly greater than that between North and South Korea.

Two other differences between the two cases are especially crucial: First, the distinctive rent-seeking structure and operation of the North Korean economy described in Chapter Three; second, North Korea's pursuit of a nuclear weapons program and other weapons of mass destruction. These differences are without counterparts in the East German-West German case.

Germany's Reunification Costs

The magnitude of resource transfers from West to East Germany—a rough indicator of the economic cost of reunification—has been enormous: about 1.4 trillion *deutsche marks* (DM) up to 2000, and over 100 billion DM per year during the first three years of the 21st century.[1] These transfers represent about 5 percent of West Germany's GDP during this period.

Unsurprisingly, this experience has been a disincentive for contemplating the costs of reunification in Korea. In turn, this disincentive has led to an often tacit inference that the costs of reunification in Korea would be relatively higher because the preunification gap between the South and North Korean economies is relatively larger than the gap between the West and East German economies. This inference is unwarranted for several reasons:

The macroeconomic policies chosen—albeit for pressing political reasons—by the FRG government at the time of German unification in 1990 directly contributed to raising the ensuing burden imposed on West Germany. Specifically, the FRG immediately established parity between the West German *deutsche mark* and the East German *ostmark,* despite the fact that the purchasing power equivalence between the two currencies was between 3:1 and 4:1.

---

[1] Bibow (2001).

Furthermore, the macroeconomic policies adopted by Germany stipulated equalizing wages, pensions, and other entitlements for workers in East and West Germany, notwithstanding the fact that measured productivity of labor in East Germany was less than one-third that of West Germany.[2] To be sure, these macroeconomic policies were adopted for strategic political considerations judged by Helmut Kohl's government to be of overriding importance regardless of the subsequent economic consequences.

Closely linked to these macroeconomic policies were the goals of economic convergence between the two German economies, goals that were stipulated to govern the reunification process and to require accelerating economic growth and raising East German per capita income to that in West Germany.

This economic convergence target highlights a key difference between the German case and the premise underlying our simulation model and our estimates of the capital costs described above. In our view, the standard for setting economic growth targets for reunification between South and North Korea should be the extremely low level of per capita GDP in North Korea and the critical importance of raising it dramatically, rather than focusing on the gap between per capita income in South Korea and North Korea. In other words, a high rate of growth of per capita income in North Korea is arguably both more appropriate and more realistic as a reunification goal. This target should be ample to motivate economic growth and macroeconomic policies in the Korean reunification process as well as more realistic than the specification of gap-elimination and economic convergence between North and South.

The standard we have adopted, rather than the "gap" standard adopted by Germany, can be justified on several grounds. First, we believe there probably is greater sensitivity in the North to the local economic plight than to the widely differing living standards and lifestyles in the South. Second, the North has been characterized by a greater insularity among its population compared to the long-

---

[2] See Sinn (2000), and Hyléen and Järvbäck (2002). North Korea's labor productivity is probably 10 percent or less of South Korea's labor productivity.

standing accessibility by the population of East Germany to conditions and living standards prevailing in West Germany. Third, we
presume that population mobility from North to South would be less
than was characteristic of the East German population's movement
toward the West.[3] It may also be pertinent to offer North Koreans
ownership rights in state-owned housing in which they live, as an inducement to remain in the North after reunification.[4]

The conclusion we draw from the preceding discussion is that
there is less about the German reunification experience that is relevant to future Korean reunification than has sometimes been assumed.

On the other hand, one aspect of the German experience may
have distinct relevance for the Korean case. Following reunification,
Germany demobilized most of the East German military forces while
allowing limited and selective absorption of some of these forces into
the unified Federal Republic's military establishment. This potentially
important aspect of the German experience has been largely ignored
in most prior research on Korean reunification.

Germany's Military Unification Experience

Here again, there are similarities and dissimilarities between the
German and Korean military circumstances prior to reunification
and, in this case too, the dissimilarities predominate.

- Prior to unification, East Germany (German Democratic Republic, or GDR) had military forces of 262,000, about 1.5 percent of the East German population of 16.6 million; the GDR's

---

[3] This is admittedly a strong and arguable assumption. In its support, we can cite the low
level of reported internal migration within North Korea compared to that in South Korea in
the 1980s, although other factors surely affect this difference (see Eberstadt and Banister,
1992). Whether or how the level of internal migration in North Korea prior to unification
relates to or foreshadows possible external migration after unification is uncertain.

[4] See Sinn and Sinn (1992).

military expenditures amounted to between 8 and 9 percent of GNP.[5]

- Currently, North Korea has approximately 1.3 million members of its regular military and reserve forces, representing about 6 percent of its population of 22.4 million, or about four times the corresponding proportion of the GDR's preunification population. North Korean military spending represents about 25–30 percent of the North Korean GDP, nearly three times the corresponding proportion in East Germany.

- While the GDR military establishment was at least moderately indoctrinated with communist ideology, the extent and intensity of indoctrination were much milder than the "Great Leader" and "Dear Leader" code of the North Korean military establishment. While selective absorption of elements of the East German military forces into the *Bundeswehr* presented serious problems, the problems would be still more acute in Korea.

- Finally, North Korea's nuclear and other weapons of mass destruction (WMD) programs, claims, or/and capabilities constitute serious and sharply dissimilar problems from those encountered in Germany. Any nuclear or other WMD precursors that may have existed in East Germany were firmly under the control of Soviet forces and exited with them.

Once the Soviet Union withdrew its objections to a unified Germany's membership in NATO, East Germany's military forces were disbanded and the *Bundeswehr* took possession of East Germany's military facilities and resources. The *Bundeswehr* created a new Eastern command that took control over all Eastern military forces, demobilizing these forces quickly and sharply (by 80 percent), retaining about 50,000 of the former East German troops and about 5,000 of the officers in the *Bundeswehr*. This was accomplished over a three-month basic training course with West German units and phased in over a two-year transitional period. All field-grade officers

---

[5] See U.S. Arms Control and Disarmament Agency (1990). Soviet military forces stationed in East Germany at the time were approximately 380,000.

were retired, as were most other officers over 55 years of age. Pension rights were retained by the demobilized military personnel.

Partly as a result of the scale and pace of demobilization and partly due to other reasons, unemployment in East Germany increased to 8.6 percent and migration from East to West Germany rose sharply in 1989 and 1990 to a total of nearly 750,000 over the two-year period, declining in the next two years to "normal" low levels.[6]

Thus, the postunification military forces of Germany were reduced from 765,000 to 335,000, or more than 55 percent, with the bulk of that reduction imposed on the former East German forces.[7] By 1997, unified Germany's military expenditures had decreased by nearly half from combined preunification military outlays ($63 billion in 1989 to $33 billion in 1997, in constant 1997 U.S. dollars). The combined military burden as a fraction of GNP in the unified Germany declined from 3.5 percent in 1991 to 1.6 percent in 1997.

Table 7.1 summarizes salient data for the two Koreas dealing with military forces and military burden to illustrate both the similarities and dissimilarities to the German data discussed above.

The problem of demobilizing the North Korean military establishment and absorbing some of it into a unified Korean military would be more formidable than in the German case. How much more will also depend on the circumstances accompanying future Korean reunification.[8]

Despite the salient differences, several implications of the German experience may be relevant to the Korean case:

- Demobilizing the bulk of North Korea's military forces expeditiously is likely to be no less important and perhaps more important than it was in Germany.

---

[6] Burda and Wiplosz (1992); and Scheremet and Zwiener (1996).

[7] In 1989, East Germany had military forces of 262,000 while West Germany had 503,000 in its military establishment.

[8] See Chapter Four.

Table 7.1
Military Forces and Military Burden in South and North Korea

Year	Military Forces (as a percent of population)		Military Expenditures (as a share of GNP)	
	South Korea	North Korea	South Korea	North Korea
1992	1.7	5.8	3.6	25
1993	1.7	5.2	3.5	25
1994	1.7	5.2	3.2	26
1995	1.7	5.1	3.0	29
1996	1.5	5.1	3.2	28
1997	1.5	5.2	3.2	28
1998	1.4	4.7	3.2	20
1999	1.4	4.7	2.9	19

SOURCE: Arms Control and Disarmament Agency (1990), U.S. Dep't of State (2002), and authors' calculat-ions and conjectures.

- The effect of rapid demobilization will tend to raise unemployment substantially in the short run, creating an urgent need for some form of economic "safety net." As noted earlier, a possibly promising solution to this problem is to demobilize the North Korean military into a Civil Construction Corps constituting a contract labor pool available for civil employment by the reunified or federalized Korean government and by private direct investors in North Korea.[9]
- To the extent that some elements of the North Korean military establishment might be absorbed into the unified military establishment, retraining and re-indoctrination of the retained former North Korean troops and officers would be critically important. Among the cardinal precepts of such retraining would be subordinating the military to a democratically elected civilian political leadership and reorienting military personnel toward a mission

---

[9] See above, pp. 43–44.

of protecting the security of the unified state rather than protecting one part of the peninsula against a threat from the other part.

- Finally, and integral to the process of reunification of the military establishments of the North and the South, is the importance of achieving resource savings from the downsizing of the two military establishments and their corresponding budgets. As reflected in our simulations, these savings should be directed to helping defray the costs of building up the capital and technology base of the North and thereby reducing the capital costs of reunification.

CHAPTER EIGHT

Conclusions: Effects on Korean Security Policies and Programs

---

The capital costs of Korean reunification will be large and burdensome, although they will probably be considerably lower and more manageable than many previous estimates have indicated. The difference between the low estimate ($50 billion) and the high estimate ($667 billion) in our simulations—a factor of 13—suggests the enormous uncertainties that would accompany reunification and its associated costs.

Managing reunification so as to constrain its associated costs requires a multifaceted strategy whose principal components include the following:

- Establishing as the key economic target of reunification a rapid rate of increase in per capita income in the North, rather than an unrealistically ambitious goal of bridging the gap between per capita income in the North and the South
- Ensuring aggressive and effective institutional reform in the unified or federated Korean state to encourage investment in the North by commercially motivated, private sources of capital both from South Korea and other international sources
- Facilitating investments with high rates of return and hence low incremental capital-output coefficients in the public as well as private sectors

- Linking the building-up of the civil capital base in the North to the building-down of the overdeveloped military establishment and military industry in the North.

Effective economic management of Korean reunification may be pursued while the reunited or federated state confronts myriad security-related problems adjacent to the economy but not disconnected from it. Two of the most prominent of these relate to weapons of mass destruction and to the bilateral or multilateral alliances that the reunified Korea might maintain, modify, or forgo. Although these problems are not the focus of this report, their importance to the report's sponsor warrants comment about them.

WMD Capabilities and Programs

However the six-power talks proceed in the future, and apart from conceivable but unlikely drastic changes in the external security environment in East Asia and elsewhere, a reunified Korean state will have strong reasons to dismantle its existing WMD capabilities as well as programs previously intended to acquire or expand them.

Motivation for this course of action derives principally from the fact that both the United States and China share strong interests in non-proliferation in general and especially in East Asia, and in precluding any possibility of Korea being a source of WMD acquisition by international terrorism. While it is possible that groups in North Korea formerly associated with WMD might be inclined to retain some residual WMD programs, at least three opposing influences would dominate such inclination. The outcome should be an early decision by a reunified Korea to terminate WMD.

First, resource constraints in the reunified state will be severe, notwithstanding our previous comments that reunification costs should be manageable; the additional costs of sustaining WMD are one reason why Korea will be disposed to comply with antiproliferation efforts.

The second and third influences leading in the same direction are the shared and strong convictions by the United States and China that retention of WMD in a reunified Korea would be regionally destabilizing and inimical to both countries' interests. Both economic considerations (the United States and China are Korea's two largest export markets) and security considerations will link the interests of a reunified Korea to the concerns and interests of China and the United States. Consequently, it seems highly probable that Korea will be disposed to cooperate with China and the United States in liquidating the prior WMD and associated programs pursued by North Korea.

One inducement to ensure WMD dismantlement would be a program along the lines of the Nunn-Lugar legislation, which has provided funding and technical assistance to accelerate nuclear dismantlement in Ukraine and other republics of the former Soviet Union, or the U.S. and EU assistance recently provided to accelerate WMD inspection and termination in Libya.

Korea's Alliance with the United States

Whether a reunified Korea will be disposed to maintain its alliance with the United States in its present form is uncertain. In particular, the reunified state is likely to be concerned that its alliance stance should give ample weight to its relations with China as well as with the United States. From this perspective, perhaps complemented by domestic political considerations within the reunified state, Korea may be inclined to favor some modifications in its alliance with the United States.

Moreover, it is also uncertain whether the United States itself will or should be disposed to maintain the alliance with Korea in its present form. Instead, an arrangement might be considered in which U.S. forces would be thinned substantially, perhaps reduced only to such minimal levels as would be useful for supporting periodic joint exercises with Korean forces. With the North Korean threat removed consequent to unification, retaining U.S. forces on the peninsula would no longer serve a symbolic or a tripwire function. Moreover, their value as part of the transformed U.S. global military posture would be less than if they were based elsewhere and reconfigured as lighter, more mobile forces, more readily and rapidly deployable for other contingencies related to the global counterterrorism war (e.g., Operation Enduring Freedom).

To be sure, major modifications in the U.S. alliance with Korea might have significant spillover effects, notably on the U.S. security alliance with Japan. Consequently, consideration of such modifications should properly give ample weight to, and be jointly developed with, Japan. The subject entails myriad complexities, including the size, character, and basing of U.S. naval and air forces in Japan; the present and future scale and composition of Japanese defense forces; host-nation support; and the multifaceted cooperation between the two close allies in the global war on terrorism. While related to the matters with which this report is principally concerned, these issues clearly extend beyond them, warranting a separate analysis.

A Simple Simulation Model for Sizing Korean Reunification Costs

The complexities and uncertainties surrounding Korean reunification are innumerable. Furthermore, data on the North Korean economy from the North Korean government are virtually nonexistent—the government ceased publishing economic statistics more than three decades ago—and data from other sources (notably those in South Korea) are often only informed conjectures. In combination, these circumstances make the task of simulating the potential capital costs of South-North reunification both formidable and inconclusive.

The model described here attempts to address this problem at a macroeconomic level, with the aim of generating a range of estimates for the capital costs of reunification. The various complexities and uncertainties referred to above and throughout this report are reflected by the range of assumed values for the parameters of the model:

1. South Korea's preunification GDP is denoted by G_s = $477 billion.[1]
2. North Korea's preunification GDP scaled to that of South Korea's GDP is $G_N = \alpha_i\, G_s$ (α_i is the scaling factor), with i = .03, .04, .05.
3. Incremental capital coefficient (ICOR) is δ_j, (j = 3, 4, 5).

---

[1] See Table 3.1, p. 11.

4. Preunification military spending in South Korea is M_s, which is scaled as a share, β_k, of South Korea's GDP: $M_s = \beta_k G_s$, ($k =$ .025, .03).
5. Postunification military spending in South Korea is a (reduced) share of South Korea's GDP, ($\beta_l = .02$).
6. Preunification military spending in North Korea is M_n, which is scaled as a share, γ_m, of North Korea's GDP: $M_n = \gamma_m G_N$, ($m =$ .25, .30).
7. γ_n is North Korea's postunification military spending share, ($n =$ .04, .05).
8. μ_o denotes the effectiveness of the market-oriented institutional reform strategy (IRS): $\mu_o = $ IRS, with ($o = 1, 2, 3$), indicating very effective, moderately effective, and relatively ineffective, respectively.
9. Finally, we specify that the target, (T_p), or goal for North Korea's postunification economy is to double its GDP in four to five years. $T_p =$ doubling North Korean GDP, with ($p = 4, 5$).
10. The capital build-up costs of unification are ($\delta 2 \alpha G_s$).
11. Annual savings realized from the military build-down in North and South Korea are, respectively, $S_n = \alpha G_s (\gamma_m - \gamma_n)$, and $S_k = G_s (\beta_k - \beta_l)$.
12. Total capital costs of doubling North Korean GDP $= C_r$, $C_r = \mu_o \delta_j 2 \alpha_i G_s - (\alpha_i G_s (\gamma_m - \gamma_n)) - G_s (\beta_k - \beta_l)$.

Several hundred runs of the model were done employing different combinations of the parameter values. Illustrative results are summarized in Table 5.2 and Figures 5.1, 5.2, 5.3, and 5.4, and the text discussion on pp. 37–42.

Possible sharing of the total reunification costs is indicated by $C_r = P_s + P_r + T_s + T_r$, comprising private capital flows from South Korea (P_s) and from the rest of the world (P_r); and public capital transfers from South Korea (T_s) and from the rest of the world (T_r), as discussed in the text, pp. 42–43 above.

Bibliography

Armacost, Michael, and Kenneth B. Pyle (2001). "Japan and Unification of Korea: Challenges for U.S. Policy Coordination." In Nicholas Eberstadt and Richard J. Ellings (ed.), *Korea's Future and the Great Powers*. Seattle: University of Washington Press with the National Bureau of Asian Research, 125–163.

Auty, Richard (ed.) (2001). *Resource Abundance and Economic Development*. Oxford: Oxford University Press.

Bae, Jin-Young (1996). "The Fiscal Burden of Korean Unification." *Joint U.S.-Korea Academic Studies* 6.

Bae, Jun Sik (2003). "Country Survey XVIII: Two Koreas' Defense Economy." *Defense and Peace Economics* 14(1), 61–83.

Bibow, Jorg (2001). "The Economic Consequences of German Unification: The Impact of Misguided Macroeconomic Policies." Annandale-on-Hudson, New York: Levy Economics Institute, Public Policy Brief No. 67.

Breen, Michael (2002). *North Korea Market Study*. CLSA Emerging Markets, online at www.clsa.com.

Buchanan, James M., Robert D. Tollison, and Gordon Tullock (eds.) (1980). *Toward a Theory of the Rent-Seeking Society*. College Station, Texas: Texas A&M University Press.

Burda, Michael, and Charles Wiplosz (1992). "Labor Mobility and German Integration: Some Vignettes." In Horst Siebert (ed.), *The Transformation of Socialist Economies*. Kiel, Germany: Kiel Institute for World Economics.

Central Intelligence Agency (1999). *Handbook of International Economic Statistics.* Washington, D.C.

China Statistical Yearbook (2003). Beijing: National Bureau of Statistics of China.

Chung, J. S.-h. (1974). *The North Korean Economy: Structure and Development.* Stanford, Calif.: Hoover Institution.

Chung, Y. H. (2003). "The Prospects for Economic Reform in North Korea and the Direction of Its Economic Development." *Vantage Point* 26(5), May 2003, 43–53.

Eberstadt, Nicholas (1996). "Financial Transfers from Japan to North Korea: Estimating the Unreported Flows." *Asian Survey* 36 (5).

_____ (2002). "The Threat from North Korea." Speech Before the American Foreign Policy Council's conference on Missile Defenses and American Security, December 18. Washington, D.C.: American Enterprise Institute.

Eberstadt, Nicholas, and Judith Banister (1992). *The Population of North Korea.* Berkeley, Calif.: University of California Press.

Eberstadt, Nicholas, and Richard J. Ellings (2001). "Assessing Interests and Objectives of the Major Actors in the Korean Drama." In Nicholas Eberstadt and Richard J. Ellings (ed.), *Korea's Future and the Great Powers.* Seattle: University of Washington Press with the National Bureau of Asian Research, 362–378.

Economist (2004). *The World in Figures 2004.* London: Profile Books Ltd.

Economist Intelligence Unit (2003). *North Korea: Country Report.* London: The Economic Intelligence Unit.

Flake, L. Gordon (1998). *North Korea and Northeast Asian Regional Integration.* Washington, D.C.: Center For Strategic and International Studies.

Frecaut, Dominique Dwor (2003). "Korean Unification: One Country, Two Systems?" In *Confrontation and Innovation on the Korean Peninsula.* Washington, D.C.: The Korea Economics Institute, 60–70.

Fujio, G. (1999). "North Korea Will Reinforce Connections with the South." *Korea's Economy* 15, 93–99.

Gianaris, Nicholas V. (1970). "International Differences in Capital-Output Ratios." *American Economic Review* 60(3), 466–477.

Harrison, S. S. (2002). *Korean Endgame: A Strategy For Reunification and U.S. Disengagement.* Princeton and Oxford, Princeton University Press.

Hersh, Seymour M. (2003). "What the Administration Knew About Pakistan and the North Korean Nuclear Program." *The New Yorker*, January 27.

Hippel, David Von, and Peter Hayes (2003). "Regional Energy Proposals and the DPRK." *Korea's Economy* 19, 61–71.

Hong, Ihk-pyo (2002). "A Shift Toward Capitalism? Recent Economic Reforms in North Korea." *East Asian Review* 14(4): 93–106.

Hong, S.-j. (2001). "Deepening Economic Cooperation with North Korea." *Korea's Economy* 17, 71–76.

Hwang, Eui-Gak (1993). *The Korean Economies: A Comparison of North and South.* Oxford, UK: Clarendon Press.

Hyléen, Charlotta, and Anna Järvbäck (2002). "Did Unification Affect the German Economy?" Lund University: Lund Macroeconomic Studies, LMS 2002:3.

International Institute for Strategic Studies (IISS) (2004). *The Military Balance 2003–2004.* London: IISS.

Jo, Dongho (1996). *The Quality of North Korean Labor and Implications for Investment in the North.* Chongyang Seoul, Korea: Korea Development Institute.

Kim, Chung-Kyun (2000). *Strategies for Investing in North Korea.* Seoul: Hyundai Research Institute.

Kim, S. W. (1994). "North Korea's Foreign Trade and the Permanent Export Hypothesis." In S. Y. Kwack (ed.), *The Korean Economy at a Crossroad.* Westport, Conn.: Praeger.

Korea Institute for International Economic Policy (2003). *North Korea Development Report.* Seoul, Korea.

Korea National Statistics Office (2002). "South and North Korean Society Through Major Statistics." News Releases, 2002.

"Korea's Economy and the Costs of Reunification" (1999). In *Patterns of Inter-Korean Relations.* Bae Ho Hahn and Chae-Jin Lee (eds.). Seoul: Sejong Institute.

Krueger, Anne (1974). "The Political Economy of the Rent Seeking Society." *The American Economic Review* 64 (3), June 1974, 291–303.

Kwan, Chi Hung (2004). "Why China's Investment Efficiency Is Low: Financial Reforms are Lagging Behind." *China in Transition,* June 18, 2004.

Lee, Chung Min, and Pollack, Jonathan D. (1999). *Preparing for Korean Unification: Scenarios and Implications.* Santa Monica, Calif.: RAND Corporation, MR-1040-A.

Lee, J.-c. (2002). "The Implications of North Korea's Reform Program and Its Effects on State Capacity." *Korea and World Affairs,* 357–364.

Lee, Joon-Koo (1995). "Reflections on Korean Unification Cost Studies." In Myoung-Kyu Kang and Helmut Wagner, eds., *Germany and Korea: Lessons in Unification.* Seoul: Seoul National University Press, 96–121.

Lee, S.-h. (2003). "North Korea's Energy Shortage and the Second Nuclear Weapons Crisis." *Vantage Point* 26(8), August 2003, 43–54.

Lee, S.-M. (1993). "A Study on Patterns of Economic Integration Between North and South Korea." *East Asian Review* 5 (3), 91–133.

Lee, Young Sun (1994). "Economic Integration of the Korean Peninsula: A Scenario Approach to the Cost of Unification." In Sung Yeung Kwack (ed.) *The Korean Economy at a Crossroad.* Westport, Conn.: Praeger.

Levin, Norman D., and Young-Sup Han (2002). *Sunshine in Korea: The South Korean Debate over Policies Toward North Korea.* Santa Monica, Calif.: RAND Corporation, MR-1555-CAPP.

Meade, Douglas S. (1997). "The Impact of Korean Unification on North Korea." College Park, Md.: University of Maryland, INFORUM Working Paper No. 97-008.

Natsios, A. (1999). *The Politics of Famine in North Korea.* Washington, D.C.: The United States Institute of Peace.

_____ (2002). *The Great North Korean Famine.* Washington, D.C.: The United States Institute of Peace.

Nautilus Institute (2000). *Northeast Asia Peace and Security Network*, Special Report, Number 6, Berkeley, Calif.: Nautilus Institute.

Newcomb, W. (2003). "Reflections on North Korea's Economic Reform." *Korea's Economy* 19, 57–60.

Noland, Marcus (1996). "The North Korean Economy." In *Joint U.S.-Korea Academic Studies*, Vol. 6.

_____ (2000). *Avoiding the Apocalypse: The Future of the Two Koreas*. Washington. D.C.: Institute for International Economics.

_____ (2001). "Famine in North Korea: Causes and Cures." *Economic Development and Cultural Change* 49(4), 741–768.

_____ (2003). "Famine and Reform in North Korea." Washington, D.C.: Institute for International Economics, WP 03-5.

Noland, Marcus, Sherman Robinson, and Li-Gang Liu (1998). "The Costs and Benefits of Korean Unification." Stanford, Calif.: Stanford University Asia/Pacific Research Center.

Noland, Marcus, Sherman Robinson, and Monica Scatasta (1996). "Modeling Economic Reform in North Korea." Washington, D.C.: Institute for International Economics, WP 96-10.

_____ (1997). "Modeling Economic Reform in North Korea." *Journal of Asian Economics* 8(1), 15–38.

Noland, Marcus, Sherman Robinson, and Tao Wang (2000). "Rigorous Speculation: The Collapse and Revival of the North Korean Economy." *World Development* 28(10), 1767–1787.

Oh, Kongdan, and Ralph Hassig (2000). *North Korea Through the Looking Glass*. Washington, D.C.: Brookings Institution Press.

Oh, Seung-yul (2003). "Changes in the North Korean Economy: New Policies and Limitations." *Korea's Economy* 19, 72–78.

Park, Sak-sam (2002). "Measuring and Assessing Economic Activity in North Korea." *Korea's Economy* 18, 76–83.

Piazolo, Mark (1997). "Could South Korea Afford German-Style Reunification?" *The Economics of Korean Unification* 2(2).

Pollack, Jonathan D., and Chung Min Lee (1999). *Preparing for Korean Unification: Scenarios and Implications*. Santa Monica, Calif.: RAND Corporation, MR-1040-A.

Reiss, M. (2002). "KEDO: Which Way From Here?" *Asian Perspective* 26(1), 41–55.

Rowen, Henry, and Charles Wolf, Jr. (1990). *The Impoverished Superpower: Perestroika and the Burden of Soviet Military Spending.* Oakland, Calif.: ICS Press.

Scalapino, R. A. (2001). "China and Korean Unification—A Neighbor's Concern." In Nicholas Eberstadt and Richard J. Ellings (ed.), *Korea's Future and the Great Powers.* Seattle: University of Washington Press with the National Bureau of Asian Research, 107–124.

_____ (2002). "Korea: The Options and Perimeters." In T. Akaha (ed.), *The Future of North Korea.* London and New York: Routledge.

Scheremet, Wolfgang, and Rudolph Zwiener (1996). "Economic Impacts of Unification." In Heiner Flassbeck and Gustav Horn (eds.), *German Unification—An Example for Korea.* Aldershott, UK: Ashgate Publishing.

Seliger, Bernhard (2004). "The North Korean Economy: Nuclear Crisis and Decline, or Peace and Reform in the Last Dynastic Asian Regime?" *Korea's Economy* 20, 77–87.

Shambaugh, D. (2003). China and the Korean Peninsula: Playing for the Long-Term, Working Paper for the Task Force on U.S.-Korea Policy sponsored by the Center for International Policy and Center for Asian Studies, University of Chicago and Brookings Institution.

Sinn, G., and H.-W. Sinn (1992). *Jumpstart: The Economic Unification of Germany.* Cambridge, Mass., and London: MIT Press.

Sinn, Hans-Werner (1996). "International Implications of German Unification." NBER Working Paper No. 5839.

_____ (2000). "Germany's Economic Unification: An Assessment After Ten Years." NBER Working Paper No. 7586.

SIPRI Yearbook: *Armaments, Disarmament And International Security* (various years). Oxford, UK: Oxford University Press.

Solomon, Jay, and Hae Won Choi (2003). "Money Trail: In North Korea, Secret Cash Hoard Props Up Regime; Defectors, Intelligence Sources Say Division 39 Supplies Billions to Kim Jong Il; Ginseng and Counterfeit Bills." *Wall Street Journal* (Eastern Edition), July 14. p. A.1.